ABOLITION &
THE UNDERGROUND
RAILROAD
in
CHESTER COUNTY,
PENNSYLVANIA

ABOLITION &
THE UNDERGROUND
RAILROAD
in
CHESTER COUNTY, PENNSYLVANIA

Mark Lanyon

THE
History
PRESS

Published by The History Press
Charleston, SC
www.historypress.com

Front cover: Longwood Progressive Friends Meetinghouse and Harriet Tubman.

Back cover: Sojourner Truth and Marlborough Meetinghouse.

First published 2022

Manufactured in the United States

ISBN 9781467150255

Library of Congress Control Number: 2016939297

This book is dedicated to the author's three grandchildren:
Hezekiah, Jemimah and Nehemiah.

In memory of Mary Larkin Dugan (1935–2013),
the founder of the Kennett Underground Railroad Center.

CONTENTS

ACKNOWLEDGEMENTS

I would like to thank the following people for their various roles in helping this book come together:

- My sister, Mary-Justine Lanyon.
- Dr. Ernest "Ernie" Levister (LU '58), whose great-grandfather was Thomas Henry Amos and whose great-grand-uncle was James Ralston Amos.
- Dr. Cheryl Gooch.
- Judy Ng from the Chester County History Center.
- Kelin Baldridge from the Chester County History Center.
- Lynn Sinclair from the Kennett Heritage Center.
- Terry Maguire from the Kennett Underground Railroad Center.
- Scott Doyle from the Pennsylvania Historical and Museum Commission.
- Taylor Reynolds from the Delaware Historical Markers Program.
- Banks Smither from The History Press.
- My wife, Beth Ann.

INTRODUCTION

The author's sister, who lives in Lake Arrowhead, California, emailed the author to say she had told a friend that her brother had graduated from Lincoln University with a Master's of Human Services (LU '98). A few weeks later, the author's sister was talking to the friend's husband, who told her he had also graduated from Lincoln and that one of his ancestors was instrumental in the founding of Lincoln. That would make an interesting story.

Later, the author's sister emailed both the author and her friend's husband as an introduction. Ernie (Dr. Ernest Levister, LU '58) and the author began emailing each other and then had Zoom meetings. As it turns out, Ernie's great-grandfather was Thomas Henry Amos, and his great-grand-uncle was James Ralston Amos. Ernie told the author that these ancestors had helped found Lincoln University. Having attended Lincoln, the author had never heard this before. This also would make an interesting story.

Seeing that they had both attended Lincoln, the author began thinking about writing a book about the facts, faces and firsts of Lincoln University. The author reached out to Dr. Cheryl Gooch and discussed this book subject with her. Dr. Gooch is the former dean of the College of Arts, Humanities and Social Sciences at Lincoln University. Her recommendation was to think beyond that subject.

The author knew Harriet Beecher Stowe was his cousin. Having lived in Southern Chester County for years, the author had heard about the Longwood Progressive Friends Meetinghouse, the Underground Railroad,

Quakers and the abolitionist movement. However, the author did not know any of the particulars. This could be an interesting story.

With that in mind, the author thought about gathering these interesting stories to create one story—and that is how this book came to be. Please join the author as he explores some of the major people, places and events of *Abolition & the Underground Railroad in Chester County, Pennsylvania.*

Note: In this book, the term freedom seeker—*short for* freedom-seeking enslaved person—*is used. This is used in place of* fugitive enslaved person, escaped enslaved person *or* runaway enslaved person. *This term better reflects who these enslaved people were—enslaved people in pursuit of freedom.*

The first chapter explores slavery and the Mason-Dixon line. Jeremiah Dixon and Charles Mason were hired by the Penn and Calvert families to determine the exact boundary line between Maryland and Pennsylvania. Mason and Dixon utilized the Stargazer Stone for their astronomical calculations, which relied on the North Star. Years later, freedom-seeking enslaved people (freedom seekers) would also rely on the North Star to guide them to freedom. As enslaved people became more aware of what going to Pennsylvania could mean—the difference between remaining in bondage versus being free to pursue a life—the draw toward the Mason-Dixon line grew. Southern Chester County, which was just across the Mason-Dixon line, became a goal for enslaved people, and in order to help them accomplish their goal of reaching freedom, the Underground Railroad was formed.

Chapter 2 examines how the Underground Railroad worked and who it helped. Kennett Square, Pennsylvania, was known as a hotbed of abolitionism. There were more Underground Railroad stations in Kennett Square and the surrounding area than anywhere else in the nation. Both White and Black people were a part of the Underground Railroad. The Underground Railroad was a grassroots movement that began in response to the repressive and oppressive laws that helped promote slavery. The many people involved with the Underground Railroad were led by one driving force: assisting freedom seekers in their pursuit of freedom.

Chapter 3 discusses the abolitionist movement. In Southern Chester County, there were a number of abolition societies and anti-slavery societies. Many progressive Quakers were both abolitionists and active members of the Underground Railroad. Three events occurred that had large effects on the abolitionist movement. The first was the kidnapping of two free Black girls from Southern Chester County. The second was the kidnapping of a Black man from his Southern Chester County home in the dead of night. The third occurred just over the Chester County line in Christiana and was known as the Christiana Riot or Resistance. These three events strengthened the resolve of the abolitionist movement.

Chapter 4 introduces the reader to the Longwood Progressive Friends Meeting (LPFM) and Meetinghouse. Progressive Quakers were tired of talk and believed action was necessary to bring about the end of slavery and to assist freedom seekers on their journeys to freedom. Many of the founding members of the LPFM had been disowned by their home meetings due to their involvement with the Underground Railroad and for holding "radical" abolitionist beliefs. LPFM hosted many famous speakers, including Frederick Douglass, Susan B. Anthony, Thomas Garrett, Sojourner Truth and Harriet Beecher Stowe. LPFM helped bring about the Reconstruction amendments. Because of its rich history, the National Park Service has designated LPFM as a historic site.

Chapter 5 talks about Hinsonville. James Ralston Amos and his brother Thomas Henry moved to Hinsonville, and they helped develop this small community. Some of the members of Hinsonville, including both James and Thomas, were active in the Underground Railroad. Some freedom seekers would assimilate into the community and were not found by the slave catchers who were looking for them.

Chapter 6 shows the development of Hosanna Meeting House, later called Hosanna Church. The Amos brothers helped build this church and were trustees of the church. It was through Hosanna and the desire for more theological training that James Ralston Amos met Reverend John Miller Dickey, who ended up tutoring James.

Chapter 7 explains when the need for an educational institution became evident. Reverend John Miller Dickey and the community of Hinsonville, led by the Amos brothers, cofounded Ashmun Institute, later renamed Lincoln University.

Appendix A lists many of the firsts of Lincoln University.

Appendix B explores the relationship between Dr. Albert Barnes, Laura Barnes, the Barnes Foundation and Lincoln University.

The motto of Lincoln University is: "If the son shall make you free, you shall be free indeed." Nothing makes this statement truer than the series of events that occurred in Southern Chester County, Pennsylvania—truly the crucible of freedom.

1

SLAVERY IN PENNSYLVANIA

This chapter is not meant to be an in-depth study of slavery in Pennsylvania. It will cover a timeline of slavery in state of Pennsylvania and will highlight events specific to Southern Chester County.

TIMELINE FOR SLAVERY IN PENNSYLVANIA

1700
Pennsylvania legalizes slavery.

1711
Pennsylvania prohibits the importation of Black people and Natives.

1712
Pennsylvania prohibits the importation of enslaved people.

1763
Charles Mason and Jeremiah Dixon are hired to locate and mark the boundary line between Pennsylvania and Maryland, which became known as the Mason-Dixon line.

1780

Pennsylvania passes the Gradual Emancipation Act.

1793

The First Fugitive Slave Law is passed, allowing slave owners to cross state lines in the pursuit of fugitives. It also made abetting runaway enslaved people a penal offense.

1820

Pennsylvania passes a personal liberty statute. This legislation is called "an act to prevent kidnapping."

1826

Pennsylvania passes an anti-kidnapping law to protect free Black people. This legislation is known as the Pennsylvania Fugitive Slave Act of 1826.

1842

Prigg v. Pennsylvania declared Pennsylvania's personal liberty laws unconstitutional.

1849

Thomas Mitchell is kidnapped.

1850

The second Fugitive Slave Law is passed.

1851

The Christiana Resistance occurs.
The Parker Sisters are kidnapped.

1852

Uncle Tom's Cabin by Harriet Beecher Stowe is published.

1857

The Dred Scott decision is passed down.

1860

Pennsylvania passes another liberty law, outlawing the use of state facilities or officials to enforce the Fugitive Slave Act of 1850.

December 31, 1862

The first "watch night" is held in anticipation of President Lincoln issuing the Emancipation Proclamation.

1863

The Emancipation Proclamation is issued by President Lincoln on January 1.

The Emancipation Proclamation is signed by President Lincoln on September 22.

Freed enslaved people increase the demand for education.

1865

The Thirteenth Amendment abolishes slavery and involuntary servitude in the United States.

SIX EVENTS OCCURRED THAT had an effect on the state of Pennsylvania, including Southern Chester County:

(1.) slavery is legalized in Pennsylvania; (2.) the Mason-Dixon line is drawn; (3.) the Gradual Emancipation Act is passed by the State of Pennsylvania in 1780; (4.) the Fugitive Slave Law of 1793 is passed; (5.) the Pennsylvania Personal Liberty Law of 1826 is passed; and (6.) the Fugitive Slave Law of 1850 is passed.

1700: PENNSYLVANIA LEGALIZES SLAVERY

Slavery was legalized in Pennsylvania in 1700. With the passage of the law legalizing slavery, there was another law passed that said enslaved people and free Black people could be tried in nonjury courts. This meant that they were no longer under the same legal protection and jurisdiction as the colonists of that time.[1]

In Chester County, slavery was never a major enterprise. The male enslaved people of Chester County were primarily involved with agricultural work. During the spring and summer, there was crop planting and harvesting to do. Often, the enslaved people worked alongside their masters, performing these tasks. Fall and winter was a time to gather firewood, as well as repair fences and outbuildings as needed. Oftentimes, the male enslaved people would accompany their owners on trips to purchase needed supplies. The female enslaved people provided domestic duties for their owners' wives. This included preparing meals, house cleaning and childcare. During harvest time, female enslaved people were known to assist in the fields.[2]

The following table represents the growth of Pennsylvania's free Black population and the decline of its enslaved population:[3]

Year	Free Black People	Total	Enslaved	Percentage of Free Black People
1790	6,537	10,274	3,737	63.62
1810	22,492	23,287	795	96.58
1820	30,202	30,413	211	99.31
1840	47,854	47,918	64	99.87
1860	56,949	56,949	0	100.00

The 1780 Registry of Slaves showed a total of 132 enslaved people lived in Southern Chester County. It can be broken down as follows: in Oxford, there were twenty-eight enslaved people; Landenberg, twenty; New London, twenty-seven; East Nottingham, twenty-six; London Britain, seventeen; New Garden, one; West Nottingham, six; London Grove, four; and Kennett Square, three.[4]

The United States Constitution was amended on January 1, 1808, and this banned the importation of enslaved people into the United States. By the time land was being purchased in Hinsonville by free Black people in the 1820s, there were few enslaved people in Pennsylvania. In 1830, a total of sixty-seven enslaved people were noted in Pennsylvania in that year's census.[5]

1764: MASON AND DIXON BEGIN SURVEYING THE MASON-DIXON LINE

The second event began in the 1600s, when English kings gave land in America to their favorite people. In 1632, King Charles I gave a large tract of land to Cecilius Calvert, who was the second Lord Baltimore and a Catholic. Calvert named the parcel of land Maryland after King Charles's wife, Henrietta Maria.[6]

Next, King Charles II granted William Penn a large parcel of land in America, which he named Pennsylvania, meaning "Penn's Woods." This unknowingly created a problem, as Calvert's northern boundary line and Penn's southern boundary line overlapped by about thirteen miles. Because of this geographic miscalculation, it was not possible for both the Penn and Calvert families to lay claim to the same territory. However, neither the Calvert nor Penn families knew of this issue until Penn was told by sea captains that Philadelphia was actually a city in Maryland. This meant that Pennsylvania's only seaport no longer belonged to the state—a situation deemed completely unacceptable by Penn.[7]

In an attempt to rectify the situation, both the Penn and Calvert families encouraged people to settle on the disputed land and to pay taxes to their respective families. This resulted in confusion, as residents did not know who they were to pay taxes to; both families told them the revenue was going to them. The legal battles continued between the two families until the king, who was tired of the physical violence taking place on the border, decided enough was enough. The king ordered a solution be found. A commission was set up, and the surveying of the disputed boundary began. The surveying was not successful, so in 1760, another survey team was appointed. This team was also not successful. In an attempt to finally resolve the issue, Penn and Calvert reached out to the Royal Observatory to obtain recommendations for surveyors who could do a better job than the local surveyors they had previously employed. The Royal Observatory gave a sound endorsement of two English surveyors named Charles Mason and Jeremiah Dixon. The Royal Observatory was familiar with the two men because they had recently completed a successful astronomical undertaking in South Africa. After a contract was approved by William Penn's and Cecilius Calvert's grandsons in 1763, Mason and Dixon came to Philadelphia to begin their task.[8]

Mason and Dixon needed to find a reference point from which they could make accurate celestial readings to help with their boundary work. Mason and Dixon determined they had found the right site on January 7, 1764. The

Left: This white quartz stone was named the Stargazers' Stone by farmers who watched Mason and Dixon reference it when making accurate celestial readings. *Author's collection.*

Right: In 1908, the Chester County Historical Society built a stone wall around the Stargazers' Stone to protect it. *Author's collection.*

site was located on John Harlan's land. It was there that Mason and Dixon spent time "reading the stars." The reference point they used was Polaris, or the North Star—the same North Star that, years later, enslaved people would use to navigate their journeys north toward freedom. Because Mason and Dixon regularly came back to this reference point, they erected a white quartz stone to mark the spot.[9] This became known as the Stargazers' Stone, so "named by the local farmers, who watched them with Mason's tripod set over the stone, checking the stars."[10]

THE STARGAZER'S STONE

The Stargazers' Stone is located 13.2 miles from the author's house. Readers will want to visit the Newlin Township/Stargazers' Stone Park. At one end of the parking area is an informative sign that briefly explains the work of Mason and Dixon and gives directions to the Stargazers' Stone.

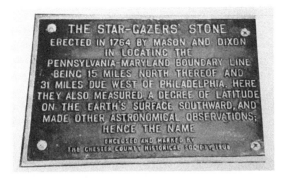

To memorialize the Harlan descendants deeding the Stargazer Stone to the Chester County Historical Society, the society placed a plaque on the stone wall it had built. *Author's collection.*

The trail to the stone is tree-lined on one side with a fence on the other. Beyond the fence is a field, where the Harlan House—the house where Charles Mason and Jeremiah Dixon stayed while working on their astronomical observations and work—is located. Following the trail, you come to the rustic four-sided stone wall that surrounds the stone.

On the front side of the enclosure is a plaque that was placed by the Chester County Historical Society in 1908. Inside the enclosure is the white quartz stone.

The Stargazers' Stone and the Harlan House are both listed in the National Register of Historical Places. The Stargazers' Stone is also designated as a National Civil Engineering Landmark, one of 125 such sites in the United States.

Newlin Township/Stargazers' Stone Park
899 Stargazer Road
Embreeville, PA 19382

~

In 1908, the descendants of the original owner of the Harlan farm, where the Stargazers' Stone was located, gave the stone and a plot of land to the Chester County Historical Society. The society built a stone wall around the stone and erected a historical marker there. The historical society deeded the site to Chester County in 1991.[11]

Upon the completion of their survey on September 11, 1768, Mason and Dixon sailed back to England. On November 9, 1768, the survey was approved by the descendants of the Calvert and Penn families. While it took England eighty-seven years to end the boundary dispute, it took only eight years for England to lose the disputed land in the American Revolution.[12]

Charles Mason and Jeremiah Dixon stayed at the Harlan House when they were in town, working on celestial readings and calculations using the Stargazer Stone. *Author's collection.*

Mason-Dixon Line

The Maryland-Pennsylvania boundary line, the Mason-Dixon line, is located 11.8 miles from the author's house. Freedom seekers who were coming from Maryland would head for this line. After entering Pennsylvania, they would head toward Hinsonville, Pennsylvania, to obtain food and rest. The next day, they would head to West Grove, Pennsylvania, to the house of Ann Preston. She would then direct or transport freedom seekers to the next station on the Underground Railroad line.

The Delaware-Pennsylvania boundary is 13.7 miles from the author's house. Freedom seekers would leave Thomas Garrett's house in Wilmington, Delaware and head north. There would be great rejoicing when they reached the Line House, which sits on the boundary between Delaware and Pennsylvania. One step over the line and they could celebrate their first taste of freedom. From the Line House, they would head a little farther north to either the Mendenhalls' house or the Coxes' house as part of the next stage of their quest for freedom.

The third event that affected Southern Chester County was the passage of the Gradual Emancipation Act of 1780 by the Pennsylvania legislature. The passage of this bill resulted in the Mason-Dixon line becoming the difference between freedom and slavery.[13] What would most likely have passed into historical obscurity became "the world's most famous boundary."[14] For freedom seekers, reaching the Mason-Dixon line, located in Chester County, was synonymous with a new life, filled with promise, freedom and self-respect.[15]

1780: Passage of the Gradual Emancipation Act

The goal of the Gradual Emancipation Act was to end slavery—but over an extended period. The main condition of this act declared that no children born in Pennsylvania after this law went into effect would be enslaved. However, if a child was born to a Black or mulatto enslaved mother, that child would be an indentured servant until the age of twenty-eight, at which time they would be emancipated. Another onerous part of this act was that all enslaved people would continue to be enslaved as long as they were registered with the state before November 1, 1780. If the owner did not register their enslaved people by this date, they would be considered free.[16]

The act of 1780 forbade citizens of Pennsylvania from possessing any new enslaved people.[17] The act of 1780 also eliminated the discriminatory regulations that had been implemented in the state over the years. The 1700 law eliminated trial by jury for both enslaved people and free Black people. The 1726 law forbade marriage between a White person and a Black person. The 1726 law also forbade Black people from meeting each other. With the passage of the act of 1780, Black people were covered by the same legislation as White people.[18]

The passage of the Gradual Emancipation Act of 1780 brought an influx of freedom seekers from neighboring states, primarily Delaware, Virginia and Maryland. Enslaved people who were yearning for freedom came to understand that Pennsylvania represented the freedom they sought. Southern Chester County became a primary destination, with freedom seekers coming from Delaware through Wilmington, Delaware, and freedom seekers coming from Maryland and Virginia through Oxford, Pennsylvania.[19]

In 1700, slavery was legalized in Pennsylvania. In 1780, the Gradual Emancipation Act was passed. In 1790, there were 3,737 enslaved people in Pennsylvania, and by 1860, there were none. Between 1790 and 1860, the percentage of free Black people grew from 63.62 percent to 100 percent.[20]

Pennsylvania realized slavery was wrong and strove to eliminate it. Citizens could relate their own war of independence to the plight of the enslaved people. As they strove to obtain freedom from the oppressive British, they, in turn, began to entertain the notion that enslaved people should be free. It took three years for the Gradual Emancipation Act to become law. In 1778, the popular opinion was that slavery should be abolished. In 1779, legislation advocating for the abolition of slavery was written. Then in 1780, Pennsylvania became the first state in the Union to approve legislation to bring about the end of slavery.[21] The abolition of slavery in Pennsylvania may not have happened as quickly as some would have liked, but the state acted and brought about the end of slavery.[22]

1793: First Fugitive Slave Act Passed

The fourth event to occur was the passage of the First Fugitive Slave Act. Although the founding fathers believed fugitive enslaved people should be returned to their owners, there were no directions in the constitution about how this was to be accomplished. It became clear that Congress needed to develop rules for the handling of freedom seekers. Shortly after this decision, the First Fugitive Slave Act was developed and passed.[23]

The Fugitive Slave Act of 1793 became law once President George Washington signed the bill. This meant that as of February 12, 1793, freedom seekers could be seized and turned over to their masters. It also meant that there were legal consequences for those who tried to prevent freedom seekers from being returned to their owners or for those who helped freedom seekers escape.[24]

The key facts about the Fugitive Slave Act of 1793 were:

- The Fugitive Slave Act of 1793 consisted of four sections, two of which dealt with the interstate extradition of accused criminals, and two of which addressed the interstate disposition of fugitive enslaved people.
- Section 3 of the Fugitive Slave Act of 1793 enabled slave owners or their agents to cross state lines to capture runaway enslaved people, take them before a federal or local magistrate and, upon presenting proof of ownership, receive authorization to return the fugitive to slavery. The law provided alleged fugitive enslaved people with no protection of habeas corpus, no right to trial by jury and no right to testify on their own behalf.
- Section 4 of the Fugitive Slave Act of 1793 made it a federal crime to aid fugitive enslaved people and established a penalty of $500 for doing so.
- The Fugitive Slave Law of 1793 put real teeth into the Constitution's Fugitive Slave Clause, but it also opened the door to potential abuses by unscrupulous slave owners and their agents.
- Fearing that the Fugitive Slave Law of 1793 encouraged slave owners to capture free Black people and present them as runaway enslaved people, some northern states enacted personal liberty laws that gave suspected fugitives judicial rights that the federal law denied them.
- In 1850, Congress replaced the Fugitive Slave Act of 1793 with an even harsher law as part of the Compromise of 1850.[25]

PENNSYLVANIA PERSONAL LIBERTY LAW
OF 1826

The fifth event was that Pennsylvania became the first northern state to pass a personal liberty law in 1820. This statute was titled the "Act to Prevent Kidnapping."[26] This law was created to prevent the kidnapping of freedom seekers who had fled to Pennsylvania in search of freedom. The Fugitive Slave Act of 1793 not only allowed slave masters and/or their agents to enter northern states to capture freedom seekers, but it also inadvertently encouraged unscrupulous slave catchers to capture free Black people to sell them into slavery. In response to these activities, the Pennsylvania Fugitive Slave Act of 1826 was passed, which was known as "an act to give effect to the provisions of the Constitution of the United States, relative to freedom seekers from labour, for the protection of free people of colour and to prevent kidnapping."[27] So, this Pennsylvania personal liberty law was meant to protect both freedom seekers and free Black people residing in Pennsylvania.

As it turned out, the Fugitive Slave Act of 1793 did not have the impact slave owners were hoping for. It appeared that a more stringent law was needed. In order to meet that need, the Fugitive Slave Act of 1850 was drafted.[28]

1850: SECOND FUGITIVE SLAVE ACT PASSED

The sixth event that occurred was the passage of the Fugitive Slave Act of 1850. Virginia senator James M. Mason wrote the Fugitive Slave Act of 1850 in response to the southern slaveholders' complaints of the ineffectiveness of the Fugitive Slave Act of 1793.[29] This new law took effect with President Millard Fillmore's signature and provided southern slaveholders with more legal cover as they crossed into northern states seeking the return of their freedom seekers.

The following are the highlights of this new law:

- The Fugitive Slave Act of 1850 was enacted by the United States Congress on September 18, 1850.
- It allowed the federal government to track down and apprehend fugitive enslaved people in the North.
- It made any federal marshal or other official who did not arrest an alleged runaway enslaved person subject to a fine of $1,000.

- It required law enforcement officials to arrest anyone suspected of being a runaway enslaved person on no more evidence than a claimant's sworn testimony of ownership.
- It denied suspected runaway enslaved people of the right to jury trials.
- It denied suspected runaway enslaved people the right to testify on their own behalf.
- It stipulated those persons who aided runaway enslaved people by providing food or shelter were subject to six months' imprisonment and $1,000 fines.
- It created a force of federal commissioners who were empowered to pursue fugitive enslaved in any state and return them to their owners.
- It empowered federal commissioners to issue warrants, depose witnesses and employ federal marshals to arrest and imprison suspected runaways within the jurisdictions of the individual states.
- It empowered federal commissioners to impose fines of $1,000 on federal marshals or local officials who did not cooperate in the pursuit or arrest alleged runaways.
- The federal commissioners employed by the Fugitive Slave Act of 1850 received ten dollars, paid by the plaintiffs (slave owners), for each suspect sent back into bondage and half of that amount for each suspect set free.
- It empowered the federal government to deputize citizens, even against their will, and force them to take part in posses or other groups to seize fugitive enslaved people.
- Historians estimate that 80 percent of accused runaways brought before federal commissioners under the Fugitive Slave Act of 1850 were sent into bondage.[30]

Many northerners disapproved of the Fugitive Slave Act of 1850 because:

- The terms of the law were much harsher and more unfair to suspected runaway enslaved people.
- The terms of the law impinged on their own freedoms by requiring them to personally participate in the pursuit and apprehension of suspected runaways.
- It circumvented state and local jurisdictions and expanded the power of the federal government.[31]

Abolitionists called the Fugitive Slave Act of 1850 the "bloodhound bill," because bloodhounds were used by slave masters and/or their slave catchers to apprehend freedom seekers. This bill was considered to be a leading factor in unrest in the country and the tension between the North and the South, and it was ultimately a major factor in the start of the Civil War.[32]

❧ ❧ ❧

As enslaved people became more aware of what going to Pennsylvania could mean—the difference between remaining in bondage and being free to pursue a life—the draw toward the Mason-Dixon line grew. At the same time, slave masters and their agents became aware of the attraction the Mason-Dixon line and pursued measures to ensure that enslaved people did not flee and, if they did, they would be captured and returned to slavery.[33] Change was taking place, and a variety of activities were contributing to this change:

> The effect of all of these activities—the antislavery legislation, the abolitionist societies, and the publications—was the creation of an atmosphere in which many people recognized the evils of slavery and developed a desire to do something about it, even at the risk of their own well-being. It was in this atmosphere that the Underground Railroad would find support and the opportunity to grow over a large portion of the United States—particularly in Pennsylvania.[34]

Southern Chester County, which was just across the Mason-Dixon line, became a goal for enslaved people, and in order to help enslaved people accomplish their goal of reaching freedom, the Underground Railroad was formed.

2

THE UNDERGROUND RAILROAD IN SOUTHERN CHESTER COUNTY

The Underground Railroad was a grassroots movement that was started in response to the repressive and oppressive laws that helped promote slavery. The many people involved with the Underground Railroad were led by one driving force: assisting freedom seekers in their pursuit of freedom. The Underground Railroad comprised a variety of different people and functions. Some were active agents who helped freedom seekers along the "line." Some ventured into the South, carrying information to enslaved people and others sympathetic to the cause. Some enslaved people never left the South, but they stayed to assist others who decided to seek freedom.[35]

Just as with a real railroad, the Underground Railroad had stations, station masters, conductors and other members—all played a role in this campaign to bring captives to freedom. This chapter will explore these people who made up the nation's first act of civil disobedience since the Revolutionary War. The second paragraph of the United States Declaration of Independence states: "We hold these truths to be self-evident, that all men are created equal, that they are endowed by their creator with certain unalienable rights, that among them are life, liberty, and the pursuit of happiness." Many people, including a number of Quakers, believed these words applied to all people in the United States—both free and enslaved.

This is why so many people in Pennsylvania opposed slavery and were willing to assist freedom seekers instead of slave owners and their agents.[36] Because members of the Underground Railroad felt that slavery and the

Fugitive Slave Acts of 1793 and 1850 were wrong, they had no hesitation ignoring these laws and assisting freedom seekers by providing food, clothing, shelter and, if needed, transportation to the next station. The most active time for the Underground Railroad was between 1835 and 1855, although there was activity prior to and after these dates.[37] It is estimated that close to fifty thousand slaves came through Chester County in their pursuit of freedom between the years 1825 and 1861.[38]

ORGANIZATION AND VOCABULARY
OF THE UNDERGROUND RAILROAD

The Underground Railroad was a railroad of sorts, although there were no tracks, official stations, railroad cars or schedules. The steam locomotive was a new invention, and the Underground Railroad utilized the concepts and nomenclature of the railroads to describe its activities.[39] So, the Underground Railroad was, in effect, a clandestine mode of transportation made up of people, both Black (former enslaved people and free Black people) and White people, male and female, who desired to assist freedom seekers succeed in their quests. The origin the Underground Railroad's name came when a group of frustrated slave catchers, who could not find their bounty, proclaimed, "There must be an underground railroad somewhere."[40]

The homes where freedom seekers would be fed, clothed and hidden were known as stations or depots, and they were safe havens fugitive enslaved people. The homeowners were known as "station masters." Freedom seekers had to be taken from station to station, and this was done by "conductors." Just like railroad organizations, stockholders were needed for the Underground Railroad. These people provided the finances to assist station masters with buying food and clothing providing and transportation for the conductors. As a rule of thumb, anyone who worked on or with the Underground Railroad fell under the broad category of "agent."[41]

Upon their arrival at a station, freedom seekers would alert station masters by knocking on a door or window. The station masters would let freedom seekers into their homes and provide them with food and a place to spend the night. If it was thought that a slave catcher was in the vicinity, freedom seekers would be hidden in a wagon and taken to the next station on the line. Many of the stations had creative places to conceal fugitives. Some houses had false walls and tunnels leading to a barn, and other station masters hid freedom seekers in their spring houses.

There were two types of conductors: the ones who assisted freedom seekers move from station to station in the North and those who assisted freedom seekers on their journey from the South to the North. The best-known conductor who assisted freedom seekers move from the South to the North was probably Harriet Tubman (she will be discussed in detail in chapter 4).

For the best protection, conductors usually transported freedom seekers overland under the protection of darkness. Some conductors also used large Dearborn wagons, which had ample space, to conceal freedom seekers from curious eyes. Some station masters involved their families in this secret operation. Sometimes, children would drive the wagons that transported freedom seekers to the next station.

To assist freedom seekers on their journeys to freedom, spirituals were sometimes sung. Singing about the Jordan River referred to the Mason-Dixon line; the "promised land" referred to Pennsylvania. The "drinking gourd" referred to the big dipper, which contains the North Star. As long as freedom seekers followed the North Star, they were headed in the right direction. It is interesting to note that the North Star held importance for two parties: Mason and Dixon to accomplish their boundary survey, which resulted in the Mason-Dixon line, and freedom seekers.[42]

One of the most influential towns and main lines on the Underground Railroad network was Kennett Square. Within and surrounding the town of Kennett Square was perhaps the largest concentration of Underground Railroad stations in the nation.[43]

The location of Kennett Square also contributed to it being such an important town on the Underground Railroad network. Freedom seekers who were coming from Delaware, Maryland and Virginia would often take the route that passed through Wilmington, Delaware, to enter Pennsylvania and go to either the Mendenhalls' or Coxes'

KENNETT SQUARE, PENNSYLVANIA

Kennett Square is located eight miles from the author's house. Kennett had a large concentration of Underground Railroad stations. The Kennett area was home to some of the best-known stationmasters, including Isaac and Dinah Mendenhall, John and Hannah Cox, Dr. Bartholomew Fussell, Eusebius and Hanna Barnard and James Walker.

For those freedom seekers who were coming from Thomas Garrett's station in Wilmington, Delaware, the Kennett Square area was the first stop on their journey to freedom.

The Underground Railroad had its beginnings in and around Southern Chester County, where Kennett Square is located.

home to begin their journey northward. These were just two of the many stations located near Kennett Square. The other popular route took freedom-seeking enslaved people from Virginia and Maryland, through Oxford, Pennsylvania, to Hinsonville and then to West Grove, where conductors would assist freedom seekers on their journeys. Later in this chapter, we will explore some of the station masters who lived in and near Kennett Square. Kennett Square was, for many freedom seekers, the first stop on their journey to freedom. This made sense, because the Underground Railroad had its beginnings in and around Chester County, where Kennett Square is located.

Of the 132 Underground Railroad agents located in Chester County, 31 were Black and 101 were White.[44] From that number of agents in Chester County, there were a minimum of 80 station masters who helped freedom seekers on their journeys.[45]

SOUTHERN CHESTER COUNTY AND THE MASON-DIXON LINE

How the Mason-Dixon line came into existence was discussed in detail in chapter 1. The Mason-Dixon line was created in order to end a decades-long dispute between the Penn and Calvert families about where the boundary line laid between Maryland and Pennsylvania. The line was completed and approved in 1768. Shortly after the Gradual Emancipation Act of 1780 was passed by the Pennsylvania legislature, Pennsylvania became a destination for fugitive enslaved people who were seeking freedom, and the Mason-Dixon line was the difference between freedom and remaining enslaved. Furthermore, the oppressive and restrictive legislation in Maryland, which began in 1796 and continued into the 1820s and 1830s, affected both free Black and enslaved people.[46] This resulted in an influx of both free Black and enslaved people and their families into the sanctuary Pennsylvania had offered since passage of the Gradual Emancipation Act of 1780.

The Mason-Dixon line became the boundary line that could make the difference between freedom and liberty and a life of misery and hopelessness. *Courtesy of the Pennsylvania Historic and Museum.*

As Jeremiah Dixon and Charles Mason were measuring the boundary line, they placed "crown stones" every five miles (each had an imprint of a crown) and boundary stones every mile (each had a "P" on one side for Pennsylvania and an "M" on the other for Maryland). Sometimes, as enslaved people were making their escapes, the skies at night would be overcast, and the North Star was not visible. Crawling along in the dark, a fortunate fugitive came across a boundary stone, and when he felt the sides, he determined the "P" side was the direction to go in. By stepping over the boundary stone, he was stepping into freedom.[47]

The North Star and the Underground Railroad

When Jeremiah Dixon and Charles Mason were surveying the boundary line between Maryland and Pennsylvania, they saw it as simply a job they were hired to do. They were hired because of their expertise. Night after night, they would gaze into the heavens and specifically focus on Polaris (the North Star). Little did they know that almost a century later, fugitive enslaved people who desired to be free would also focus on the North Star. Little did they know that the boundary line that became known as the Mason-Dixon line would be a line that made the difference between freedom and liberty and a life of misery and hopelessness.

Most freedom seekers did not have access to a horse, wagon or carriage to make the journey northward, which meant they had to walk. But how would a freedom seeker know what direction to take, as virtually none of them owned a compass or had ever seen an atlas? Instead, they learned about navigation from two sources: older enslaved people who had been taught about navigation and conductors who had come south to assist freedom seekers. There were also instructional songs sung by slaves, one of which was called "The Drinking Gourd."

"The Drinking Gourd" talked about the Big Dipper. There are two stars in the Big Dipper that point to the North Star (Polaris). The North Star is called such because it is always pointing due north; therefore, freedom seekers knew which direction to go during their escape by following the North Star. So, the North Star became a light in the darkness and a spotlight toward freedom. As knowledge of it grew among the slave population, there was more of an understanding of navigation that included roads and railroads that went north. These could be more reliable methods of travel, but at times, they were more dangerous because they were out in the open, unlike forests and fields. Being out in the open, freedom seekers risked being seen and caught by slave catchers.

Freedom seekers knew about the North Star—and so did their owners. Slave owners despised the North Star and stated, "If they could, they would tear it from its place in heaven."[48] Freedom seekers came to understand that if they followed the North Star, they would reach the Jordan River (the Mason-Dixon line) and could step into the promised land (Pennsylvania). From there, they could get on the train to freedom.

Early on, this train to freedom did not have a name, but it eventually became known as the Underground Railroad. Kennett Square became known as the central station and terminal for those freedom seekers who desired to come aboard. While traveling north, following the North Star and crossing the Mason-Dixon line, fugitives could be assured that conductors would lead them to stations where station masters would feed them, clothe them, provide them with shelter and either connect them to another conductor or take them on the next leg of their journey toward freedom.

LOCAL AGENTS FOR THE UNDERGROUND RAILROAD

Thomas Garrett

Thomas Garret was a founding member of the Longwood Progressive Friends Meeting.[49] Thomas Garrett's place of residence was located at Third and Shipley Streets in Wilmington, Delaware, a city about six miles south of the Mason-Dixon line. Garrett's Underground Railroad station was the first stop on the Wilmington, Delaware line for freedom seekers who were coming from Delaware, Maryland and Virginia.[50] Garrett was a key player in the Underground Railroad, and his house was the only major station south of the Mason-Dixon line. Garrett never tried to convince an enslaved person to escape; however, if an enslaved person requested assistance, he was quick to provide it.[51]

Garrett never physically took freedom seekers on the road to freedom. His primary role, which was an important one, was to provide food and shelter for the many enslaved people who had traveled for miles to reach Wilmington and needed rest and sustenance to regain their strength for the rest of their journey. Once these enslaved people were ready to continue, Garrett would explain the route they needed to take in order to reach the Pennsylvania border. Then there were times he would hire local Black men to take the freedom seekers to the Delaware line and into Pennsylvania, where they could connect with an Underground Railroad station there.[52] Some of these men included Comegys Munson, Severn Johnson, Harry Craig and Joseph Walker. These men, along with Thomas Garrett, were responsible for transporting close to three thousand freedom seekers to the Mason-Dixon line so that they could continue their journey to freedom.[53]

The instructions given to the freedom seekers were to cross the Mason-Dixon line and continue to Isaac and Dinah Mendenhall's place, just a short distance over the Pennsylvania border and ten miles from Kennett Square. Sometimes, Garrett would receive word that the slave catchers were keeping watch on the Mendenhalls, so he would send the freedom seekers to John and Hannah Cox's home. If that was not a possibility, then the Darlingtons, Chandler and Hannah, were called on to assist. These three couples worked closely together to ensure the safety of those seeking freedom.[54]

Thomas Garrett had the only major Underground Railroad station south of the Mason-Dixon line, and he assisted more than 2,700 enslaved people on their journey to freedom. *Courtesy of the Chester County History Center.*

Both Thomas Garrett and his wife were creative in the way they assisted freedom seekers escape Wilmington, Delaware. One time, Garrett had an enslaved woman wear one of his wife's dresses and bonnet as he escorted her from the house. The constable who was watching the house for this female freedom seeker thought they were the Garretts and wished them a good day. Then, there was the time Garrett's wife disguised herself as an enslaved woman and "fled" out the back door. The constable was looking for a freedom seeker and started to chase after her. In the meantime, the real enslaved woman went out the front door, on her way to freedom.[55] Another time, an enslaved woman arrived at Garrett's house and told him her master was close behind. At Garrett's direction, the woman clothed herself with one of Garrett wife's dresses and a hat. Together, Garrett and the female freedom seeker left through the front door and proceeded past the mystified slave owner, who was trying to figure out what had happened to his enslaved woman.[56]

Then there were times Garrett would dress a freedom seeker in clothes that made them resemble a working free Black person. He would give the freedom seeker a farm tool and have them walk toward the Delaware-

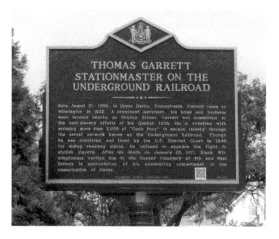

Thomas Garrett was so revered by the Black community in Wilmington, Delaware, that he was called "our Moses." *Courtesy of the Delaware Public Archives Historical Marker Program.*

Pennsylvania border. Because there were often free Black people walking to and from farm jobs, the freedom seekers did not raise suspicions. There was a designated spot to leave the tools, and later, Garrett would retrieve them in order to give them to another freedom seeker to carry out this subterfuge.[57] These examples show just how committed Thomas Garrett and his wife were to the Underground Railroad and the cause of freedom.

Garrett's approach to being involved with the Underground Railroad was that there were two sets of laws: God's laws and the laws created by man. He felt that if a law created by man was contrary to God's law, he needed to be true to himself and God and follow God's law.[58] As a Quaker, he believed he was following the light within himself, and assisting freedom seekers who asked for help was a calling placed on him.

Because of this calling, Garrett was not afraid of slave owners or slave catchers. One time, a slave owner showed up at Garrett's store in Wilmington. This slave owner was looking for a freedom seeker and believed Garrett had played a part in their escape. Frustrated that he could not find the fugitive, the slaveowner told Garrett, "If we ever catch you in our part of the world, we will tar and feather you." Later, Garrett was close to where the slaveowner lived, so he stopped in to see the man. When the slaveowner answered the door, Garrett greeted the man by saying, "Thee said thee wanted to see me when I was in this part of the world, and here I am." The slave owner could not believe what he was hearing and seeing. He told Garrett to leave and said he would make sure nobody would bother him in the future.[59]

Thomas Garrett was a founding member of the Longwood Progressive Friends Meetinghouse.[60] As a stationmaster working from the only major station south of the Mason-Dixon line, Garrett was able to assist more than 2,700 slaves on their journey to freedom. Garret was so revered and esteemed by the Black community in Wilmington that he was called "our Moses" as a sign of honor.[61] Furthermore, many people thought Garrett would be killed because of his outspoken opposition to slavery, as well as his less-than-clandestine Underground Railroad activities. Because of this, Black people would take turns at sentry duty, vowing to protect the man who meant so much to them and who had done so much for their people.[62]

Chandler and Hannah Darlington

Although Chandler and Hannah Darlington were not regular stationmasters, they cared about the safety and well-being of freedom seekers. Hannah was a founding member of the Longwood Progressive Friends Meeting, and as such, both she and her husband were known in Kennett Square as sympathizers and supporters of the freedom seekers.[63]

The location of their home was not conducive to large-scale Underground Railroad activity. However, conductors would bring freedom seekers to their home, where they would be fed and given clothing if they needed it. Shortly after this, the freedom seekers would be placed into a wagon and transported to a safer station or depot, such as the Mendenhalls' or Coxes' home.

Top: Chandler Darlington would place freedom-seeking enslaved people in his wagon and transport them to a safer station, such as the Mendenhalls' or Coxes'. *Courtesy of the Chester County History Center.*

Bottom: Hannah Darlington would feed and provide clothing for freedom-seeking enslaved people. Hannah was a founding member of the Longwood Progressive Friends Meeting. *Courtesy of the Chester County History Center.*

Ann Preston, MD

Ann's father, Amos Preston, was a founding member of the Longwood Progressive Friends Meeting.[64] Ann's home in West Grove, Pennsylvania, was a major station on the Underground Railroad branch coming from Maryland and Virginia through Oxford, Pennsylvania. Ann's home was only 11.8 miles from the Mason-Dixon Line. Creativity seems to have been a major feature of Underground Railroad members. One time, Ann needed to transport a freedom seeker, so she dressed her like a Quaker and took her in her carriage. The two of them encountered slave catchers, who, seeing who they thought were two Quaker ladies out for a ride, left them alone.[65]

Ann helped start the Female Medical College of Pennsylvania and was a member of the first graduating class. Her uncle Dr. Bartholomew

Left: Ann Preston's home was only 11.8 miles from the Mason-Dixon line and was an active station on the Underground Railroad. *Courtesy of the Pennsylvania Historic and Museum.*

Right: Aside from being active in the Underground Railroad, Ann Preston helped found the Female Medical College of Pennsylvania. *Courtesy of the Chester County History Center.*

> The home of Ann Preston is located 1.5 miles from the author's house. Ann's house was a major station on the Underground Railroad. As a medical doctor, she was able to provide medical care to freedom seekers, along with food and shelter. She would often transport her visitors to the next station on the Underground Railroad line.

Fussell of Kennett Square, a prominent abolitionist and a member of the Underground Railroad, sat on the board of the college Ann helped found. In spite of her private medical practice, she was very active in the Underground Railroad.

Isaac and Dinah Mendenhall

Isaac and Dinah Mendenhall were founding members of the Longwood Progressive Friends Meeting.[66] The Mendenhalls were among the most prominent abolitionists in the Kennett Square area. They were also key members of Underground Railroad. Their home was the closest station to the Delaware state line. A majority of the freedom seekers the Mendenhalls assisted were sent by Thomas Garrett in nearby Wilmington, Delaware. Garrett instructed the freedom seekers to "go on and on until they came to a stone gate and then turn in." They would then hand the Mendenhalls a note, stating, "I send you three [or whatever the actual number was] bales of black wool."[67] This was a coded message from Thomas Garrett so that the Mendenhalls would know they were actually sent by Garrett.

Like other station masters, the Mendenhalls used ingenuity and creativity to deal with dangerous situations. One time, a freedom seeker was in Dinah's kitchen, getting ready to have a meal. Dinah had been baking bread, and the oven was in the process of cooling down. At that moment, two slave hunters approached the house and began pounding on the door. Dinah realized she had no time to send the freedom seeker to one of the regular hiding places available on the property. So, she took the freedom seeker and placed him in the hot oven. Dinah then welcomed the slave hunters into the house and waited while they searched the premises. Finding nothing, they left. Dinah raced over to the oven and let the freedom seeker out. Although he was warm, he was not in the hands of the slave

Above, left: Isaac Mendenhall worked closely with Thomas Garrett in assisting freedom-seeking enslaved people continue their journeys to freedom. *Courtesy of the Chester County History Center.*

Above, right: Dinah Mendenhall was known and loved by the Black community. She was known as "Aunt Dinah" and worked tirelessly to care for freedom-seeking enslaved people. *Courtesy of the Chester County History Center.*

Left: Both Isaac and Dinah Mendenhall were founding members of the Longwood Progressive Friends Meeting (LPFM). *Courtesy of the Pennsylvania Historic and Museum.*

hunters, and he could finish his meal before continuing his journey on the Underground Railroad.[68]

One of the reasons the Mendenhalls worked so closely with Thomas Garrett on the Underground Railroad and with the abolitionist movement was that Isaac's sister, Rachel, was married to Thomas Garrett. Just as Thomas Garrett was given the moniker "our Moses," Isaac Mendenhall was called "Uncle Isaac," and Dinah was known as "Aunt Dinah."[69]

In 1851, John Greeleaf Whittier said of the Mendenhalls:

Whenever and wherever the cause of freedom needed aid and countenance, you were sure to be found with the noble band of Chester County men and women to whose mental culture, moral stamina, and generous self-sacrifice I can bear empathetic testimony.[70]

John and Hannah Cox

John and Hannah Cox were founding members of the Longwood Progressive Friends Meeting.[71] The Coxes were well-known abolitionists and were very active in the Underground Railroad. They worked

closely with Thomas Garrett, as well as the Mendenhalls. The Coxes' house was two miles north of the Mendenhalls' and four miles from the Delaware-Pennsylvania line.

Left: John Cox was the first president of the Kennett Anti-Slavery Society and was active in the Underground Railroad. *Courtesy of the Chester County History Center.*

Below: Hannah Pierce Cox would welcome freedom-seeking enslaved people into her home and provide them with food, shelter and clothing. *Courtesy of the Chester County History Center.*

Thomas Garrett would instruct freedom seekers to go to the Coxes' house, which was easy to find because it was on the main road that led from Wilmington, Delaware, to Kennett Square, Pennsylvania. Freedom seekers would either travel on foot or were transported by wagon. If they were transported by wagon, the conductor (who was often a Black man by the name of Jackson) would drop them off and knock on a window or fence to alert the Coxes that they had "friends."[72] The freedom seekers would be welcomed into the house and given food and clothing. If it was deemed safe, they would spend the night and be taken to another station the next day. If it was not safe, they would be taken to a new station that evening.

Both John and Hannah Cox were active in the Free Produce Movement (this will be discussed in the next chapter)—a movement that began to protest material made by slave labor.

Dr. Bartholomew Fussell

Dr. Bartholomew and his wife, Rebecca, were founding members of the Longwood Progressive Friends Meeting.[73] Dr. Fussell was one of the most active Underground Railroad stationmasters in Southern Chester County. Because of his efforts, over two thousand slaves were assisted on their journeys to freedom.[74] Abolitionism and the Underground Railroad ran in Dr. Fussell's family. Two of his nieces, Ann Preston and Graceanna Lewis, were both ardent abolitionists and were active in the work of the Underground Railroad.

Dr. Fussell was active in two antislavery societies: the American Anti-Slavery Society, of which he was a founding member, and the Pennsylvania Anti-Slavery Society.[75] The Anti-Slavery Convention was held in Philadelphia in 1833. Dr. Fussell was one of the sixty-two delegates in attendance and was a signer of the "Declaration of Sentiments."[76] At one point, Dr. Fussell had the opportunity to address the Medical Society of Baltimore. During his talk, he spoke out against slavery and told the audience he thought slavery was

It is estimated that Dr. Bartholomew Fussell assisted over two thousand freedom-seeking enslaved people on their journey to freedom. *Courtesy of the Chester County History Center.*

"preposterous and cruel" and longed for the day "when slavery…should have no abiding place in the whole habitable earth." Seeing that Maryland was a slave state, this speech was not well received.[77]

Dr. Fussell received his medical training in Maryland. He was a schoolteacher during the day and attended medical school in the evening. It was during this time Dr. Fussell began a Sunday school for enslaved people. He sometimes had as many as ninety enslaved people in attendance.[78] Once he moved to Kennett and became active in the Underground Railroad, he began having freedom seekers come to his house. On many occasions, both the freedom seekers and Dr. Fussell recognized each other—student and teacher from the Sunday school in Maryland.[79] Oftentimes, a free Black man by the name of Davy transported freedom seekers from Thomas Garrett's station to Dr. Fussell's safe haven.[80]

Enoch Lewis

Enoch was active in the abolitionist movement and the Underground Railroad. With the passage of the Fugitive Slave Act of 1793, slave owners and slave catchers were allowed to enter free state of Pennsylvania to capture freedom seekers. However, this act also emboldened less-than-honest slave catchers to kidnap free Black people. This was accomplished by slave catchers providing falsified documents to the courts, claiming free Black people were actually enslaved. These captured "enslaved people" were not allowed to have a jury trial or testify in court.

Fortunately for many free Black people who were captured and brought before a justice of the peace, Enoch knew the law and would make sure the justice of the peace understood what was actually happening and that the "enslaved person" was, in reality, a free person.[81]

Enoch's house was an active station on the Underground Railroad. His house was located in New Garden, which was close to West Grove and the Mason-Dixon line. When freedom seekers were brought to his house, he was glad to provide food, clothing and shelter. Enoch had transportation ready to move freedom seekers to a safer station if slave catchers were known to be lurking in the neighborhood.

As an advocate and friend of Black people, Enoch was always willing to do what was necessary to provide assistance. A prime example of this is when a Black woman came to Enoch's house late one night. After answering the door, Enoch recognized her as a nearby neighbor. She informed Enoch that her husband had been kidnapped by slave hunters and that he was being taken to the West Chester justice of peace. She told Enoch that she was terrified her husband would be returned to slavery. Enoch went to the justice of the peace, only to find that the case against the captured man proved valid, and he was to be returned to his owner. With no legal recourse left, his only option was to purchase the man for the sum of $400. Even though Enoch only made $500 a year, he went ahead and paid the money. The man returned to his grateful wife. Over time, he was able to pay Enoch back.[82]

Being academically minded, Enoch became a teacher at the Westtown Friends School. One time, a freedom seeker ended up spending time at Enoch's house. After Enoch learned that the man had successfully fled the South, Enoch thought his students might benefit from hearing his story. This man, however, did not show up at Enoch Lewis's home alone. He brought with him his young nephew, whom he left under the care of Enoch. After being raised by Enoch and reaching the age of eighteen, the young man left and began working and earning a living. This is an example of how much Enoch cared for the well-being of freedom seekers and their families.[83]

Enoch Lewis's one son, Joseph, followed in his father's footsteps and was a staunch advocate of the antislavery movement. Joseph was an attorney, and his expertise was needed following the Christiana Riot (which will be discussed in detail in the next chapter). Following this resistance event, an innocent Quaker by the name of Castner Hanway, who had been at the site of the incident, was erroneously charged with treason.[84] Joseph and three other attorneys pleaded Hanway's case before the courts and won. Hanway was acquitted.[85]

Joseph Lewis continued his legal career, served as the second Internal Revenue Service (IRS) commissioner and remained faithful to the cause of antislavery.

Moses and Mary Pennock and Son Samuel Pennock

Moses and Mary Pennock were founding members of the Longwood Progressive Friends Meeting.[86] Moses and Mary were ardent abolitionists and active participants in the Underground Railroad. It was their son Samuel who was the most active in the Underground Railroad and as an abolitionist. Samuel lived in Kennett Square, and his home was one of the many Underground Railroad stations located in Kennett Square. After the kidnapping of the Parker sisters (which will be discussed in the next chapter), it was discovered that one of the rescuers was Samuel Pennock.

Top: Moses and Mary Pennock were founding members of the LPFM, ardent abolitionists and active in the Underground Railroad. *Courtesy of the Chester County History Center.*

Bottom: Samuel Pennock was a staunch abolitionist, active in the Underground Railroad and a friend of free Black people and freedom-seeking enslaved people. *Courtesy of the Chester County History Center.*

Moses and Mary Pennock's house was a station on the Underground Railroad. They worked closely with their son, Samuel, in assisting freedom-seeking enslaved people. *Courtesy of the Chester County History Center.*

The following is an excerpt from an article from the *Daily Local News* (1903) that was published after the death of Samuel Pennock:

> *While Mr. Pennock helped so vigorously the industrial needs of the community, he and his wife have stood for all the great reforms of the day with unflinching and persistent aggressiveness, and their home has always stood in wide open hospitality to the advocates of the progressive movements. From the establishment of the Longwood Society of Progressive Friends, they have given munificently of their time, spirit, money and hospitality. Samuel Pennock was an ardent abolitionist at the start of the movement, a warm friend of the slave, and an officer in the Underground Railroad.... Losing his birthright membership in the Society of Friends by disownment because of his affiliation with the Longwood Progressive Movement he, however, requested and was admitted into the Membership of the Society a few years ago and was active in the duties of and faithful in his attendance upon the meetings.*[87]

Mahlon and Mary Kent Brosius

Mahlon and Mary Kent Brosius lived on a farm located near the Octoraro Creek in Upper Oxford Township, one of the stations along the Underground Railroad. Along with farming, Mahlon had a successful pottery business, which was an integral part of the Brosiuses' commitment to the Underground Railroad and the cause of assisting freedom seekers on their journeys. Two of the Brosiuses' sons, Edwin and Daniel, also assisted with Underground Railroad activities.[88]

Mahlon's earthenware pottery was in high demand, and Mahlon or one of his sons would deliver the earthenware jugs, pots and crocks throughout Chester and Lancaster Counties. Having a legitimate pottery business and needing to use horses and wagons to deliver their in-demand product provided a perfect cover when transporting freedom seekers.

However, a situation occurred that required quick thinking on the part of Daniel and Edwin. Early one evening, around 1842, thirty-three freedom seekers were brought to the Brosius home. The freedom seekers were fed and given shelter, and plans were made for their transportation. The following evening, Edwin and Daniel prepared them for the next leg of their journey. Children and women were covered with hay and hidden between the two wagons that were usually used to deliver Brosius earthenware. The men walked behind the wagons.[89]

En route to the next station, the brothers saw in the distance light from a lime kiln. Concerned the kiln workers might wonder why the wagons were out so late and why Black men were walking behind them, the brothers changed plans. The Black men were given instructions on how to travel around the kiln and were told where to meet up with the wagons. The two wagons continued on the road past the kiln but at a considerable distance apart. The freedom seekers were delivered safely to the next station.[90] When Edwin Brosius shared this story, he was quick to point out, "I and my brother, two boys, were the only White persons on the train."[91]

Eusebius and Hanna Barnard

Eusebius and his first wife, Sarah, were founding members of the Longwood Progressive Friends Meeting.[92] Abraham Lincoln was Eusebius's third cousin once removed.[93] Freedom seekers were sent to Eusebius by Thomas Garrett, the Mendenhalls, the Coxes and Dr. Fussell. Once they

Top: Abraham Lincoln was Eusebius Barnard's third cousin once removed. He and his whole family were active in the Underground Railroad. *Courtesy of the Chester County History Center.*

Bottom: Hanna Barnard and her husband, Eusebius, were founding members of LPFM. Hanna encouraged her children to participate in the Underground Railroad. *Courtesy of the Chester County History Center.*

arrived, they were fed and allowed to rest for a while. Usually in the middle of the night, they were taken to another station either by Eusebius or one of his children.

The Barnard family were staunch abolitionists. They raised money for the abolitionist movement through "bake sales, where they sold 'Barnard Cake' or 'Abolition Cake.'"[94]

The following are a few stories about Eusebius and how his children were active participants in the Underground Railroad.

One time, when Eusebius was away on a business trip, his wife asked their daughter Elizabeth to conduct some freedom seekers who had arrived the previous night to another station. Another time, neither of the parents were home—only two daughters and a young son, Enos. Seventeen freedom seekers arrived at the house and needed to be transported to another safe station. Enos was familiar with his uncle William's residence and volunteered to escort the men. After saddling up, Enos had the men follow him and proudly delivered them to his uncle.[95]

Another time, a group of freedom seekers numbering under ten arrived at the Barnard house. Eusebius was not home, and the rest of the family was about to leave for Quaker meeting. This time, Eusebius R. was charged with taking them to the next safe station. Since it was Sunday and there was a "negro quarterly meeting" underway, Eusebius R. had some of the freedom seekers ride in a wagon, and he had another drive the horses. The rest of the freedom seekers walked behind the wagon at a distance. Eusebius R. rode his horse in front to keep an eye out for potential trouble. Since it was meeting day, there were quite a few people traveling; however, nobody suspected that the freedom seekers were not on their way to their own meeting.[96]

Eusebius Barnard's home was an active station on the Underground Railroad. It is estimated that he and his family assisted hundreds of freedom-seeking enslaved people. *Author's collection.*

～

THE HOME OF EUSEBIUS AND HANNA BARNARD

The home of Eusebius and Hanna Barnard is located 12.8 miles from the author's home. Eusebius and Hanna Barnard were abolitionists and active in the Underground Railroad. Their home was one of the stations on the local Underground Railroad route.

Eusebius and Hanna, along with their family, were part of the informal society that included abolitionism, the Underground Railroad and the Longwood Progressive Friends Meeting. This informal society worked to assist freedom seekers who were wishing to make their journey to freedom.

716 South Wawaset Road
Pocopson, PA 19366
This home is not open to the public at this time.

～

Prior to the construction of the Longwood Progressive Friends Meetinghouse, the land had to be prepared. A group of friends, including Eusebius Barnard, were working on the land when eleven freedom seekers arrived, having been sent by Thomas Garrett. They waited at Longwood while the men continued with their work. With the work completed for the day, Eusebius brought the freedom seekers to his house. As was the custom, they were fed and allowed to rest until early in the morning. Eusebius R. was the conductor this time, and he safely took them to the next station. There were many thanks given for the near-miraculous trip that had just occurred, as it was only 8:00 p.m. the previous night when the freedom seekers had escaped from the Maryland plantation where they were enslaved.[97]

As with other Underground Railroad stationmasters, it is not known exactly how

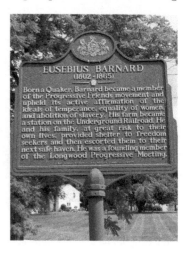

Eusebius Barnard was a Quaker, a staunch abolitionist and a friend of freedom-seeking enslaved people. *Courtesy of the Pennsylvania Historic and Museum.*

many freedom seekers were assisted by the Barnards on their journeys to freedom. However, the estimate is that hundreds came to Eusebius and his family for help.

LOCAL BLACK AGENTS AND CONDUCTORS

Many free Black agents/conductors were essential in the success of the Underground Railroad in Southern Chester County. From the little town of Hinsonville, there were a number of Underground Railroad agents: James Amos, Thomas Amos, Samuel Glasgow, Emory Hinson, Albert Walls, George Walls and William Walls. Of the 132 Underground Railroad agents active in Chester County, 31 were Black.[98] The following are some of their stories.

Harriet Tubman

The most famous and well-known Black Underground Railroad conductor is Harriet Tubman. Harriet was born into slavery in Maryland. At various points, she worked in the fields, in the woods cutting lumber and on the docks. These experiences helped her hone the skills she would need on the Underground Railroad. She learned the ways of the fields and woods, she learned about the North from the Black sailors who worked on the docks and she began setting up a network that she would later utilize as she covertly traveled between the South and the North, conducting enslaved people to their freedom.

It is estimated that she made nineteen journeys into the South to lead over three hundred enslaved people to freedom. She would let the enslaved know it was time to meet up with her by singing "I am Bound for the Promised Land" or "Swing Low, Sweet Chariot."[99]

She utilized two main Underground Railroad routes that ran through Southern Chester County. The first came up through Wilmington, Delaware, and by Thomas Garrett's house. The second came up through Oxford, Pennsylvania, by Hosanna Meeting House, and then on to West Grove, Pennsylvania. Harriet worked with Thomas Garrett when she was leading the enslaved through Wilmington, Delaware. The Black community in Wilmington referred to Thomas Garrett as "our Moses," and the slaves in the South called Harriet Tubman "Moses." Tubman often sought Garrett's

In 1982, Harriet Tubman was recognized by the Smithsonian Institute "as the only American woman ever to plan and lead a military raid." *Courtesy of the Library of Congress.*

counsel concerning the Underground Railroad. Garrett was familiar with Tubman's many close encounters as she traveled back and forth between the South and Wilmington. At one point, Garrett shared his concern when he wrote: "There is now much more risk on the road than there has been for several months past....Yet, as it is Harriet, who seems to have a special angel to guide her on her journey of mercy, I have hope."[100]

An accident occurred early on in Harriet's life that seemed to create the "angel" that Thomas Garrett wrote about. Harriet and the plantation cook went to the local store to buy supplies. They were about to enter the store when an enslaved man ran out, followed by his overseer. Hoping to stop the enslaved man, the overseer threw a weight at him. But instead of hitting its intended target, the weight crashed into Harriet's head, critically injuring her. The injury, which Harriett took a long time to recover from, resulted in Tubman experiencing "headaches, seizures, and sleeping spells—possibly temporal lobe epilepsy—that affected her for the rest of her life."[101]

Her angel came when she slipped into unconsciousness. She would have dreams that would direct her on how to travel along a particular Underground Railroad route. One time, she was escorting some freedom seekers when she experienced unconsciousness. Not knowing which direction to go in, the freedom seekers waited for her to wake up. After waking up, she shared a dream she had in which slave hunters were waiting for them on their current path. She took them in a different direction, only to find out later that there indeed were slave hunters waiting for them on their original path.[102]

Harriett Tubman and Thomas Garrett worked closely together. Harriett would stop in Wilmington so that she and her charges could receive food, shelter and rest before completing their journey to freedom. One time, Garrett said Harriet was like a Quaker, in that she appeared to rely on the "inner light" to guide her. She told Garrett, "God will preserve me from harm in all my journeys, 'cause I never go anywhere without His consent."[103]

A story is told about the first time Harriet Tubman crossed into freedom. She was traveling from Wilmington, Delaware, and came to the Line House, where the boundary line between Delaware and Pennsylvania crosses through the middle of the house. When Harriett stepped over the line, into the free state of Pennsylvania, it is reported she said: "I had crossed the line of which I had so long been dreaming. I was free. I looked at my hands to see if I was the same person, now I was free....There was such glory over everything. The sun came like gold through the trees and over the fields, and I felt like I was in Heaven."[104]

The boundary between Delaware and Pennsylvania runs through the Line House. freedom-seeking enslaved people knew they were free when they passed this house. *Author's collection.*

Although Harriett Tubman is well known for her amazing work as a conductor on the Underground Railroad, she is less known for her military duty. Her work with the Union army began when she provided nursing care to Black soldiers and freed people. Since she was familiar with the

South—and having developed communication networks during her intense Underground Railroad work—she was able to spy on the Confederate army. In early 1863:

> *She became the first woman to command an armed military raid when she guided Col. James Montgomery and his Second South Carolina Black Regiment up the Combahee River, routing Confederate forces, destroying stockpiles of cotton, food, and weapons, and liberating over 750 slaves.*
>
> *She witnessed the famed battle of Fort Wagner in Charleston Harbor, where the Massachusetts 54th Regiment fought so valiantly and demonstrated the courage and military skills of black troops.*[105]

Harriett Tubman was well known and respected for her valiant work with the Underground Railroad and the Union army. In honor of Tubman's work, Queen Victoria sent her a silver medal, along with an invitation to come to England (which Harriett never accepted). In 1982, Harriett Tubman was recognized by the Smithsonian Institute "as the only American woman ever to plan and lead a military raid."[106]

In 1914, the citizens of Auburn, New York (the town Harriet retired to), erected a memorial in her honor. The plaque on the memorial reads:

> *In Memory of Harriet Tubman*
> *Born a slave in Maryland about 1821*
> *Died in Auburn, N.Y. March 10th, 1913.*
>
> *Called the "Moses" of her people,*
> *during the Civil War, with rare*
> *courage, she led over three hundred*
> *negroes up from slavery to freedom,*
> *and rendered invaluable service*
> *as nurse and spy.*
>
> *With implicit trust in God,*
> *she braved every danger and*
> *overcame every obstacle withal*
> *she possessed extraordinary*
> *foresight and judgment so that*
> *she truthfully said—*

"On my Underground Railroad,
nebber run my train off de track
and nebber los a passenger."

This tablet is erected
by the citizens of Auburn
1914[107]

The Harriett Tubman Underground Railroad National Historical Park and Visitor Center, located in Cambridge, Maryland, is a great place to visit to learn all things Harriett Tubman. The visitor center has many displays and videos showcasing the life and legacy of Harriett Tubman. The park covers such places as the Brodess Farm, Scott's Chapel, Bazel Church, Bucktown Store, Jacob Jackson home site, Stewart's Canal and the Anthony Thompson Home site.

The address for the park and visitor center is:

4068 Golden Hill Road
Church Creek, MD 21622
410-221-2290

The Harriet Tubman Underground Railroad National Historical Park and Visitor Center is very informative and worth the visit. *Author's collection.*

James Walker

James Walker was a Black man who lived in Kennett Square. He was active in the Underground Railroad and often worked with Thomas Garrett. There is one story that exemplifies his heart when it came to assisting his fellow man.

A young, enslaved person was able to escape from Maryland. A train engineer who was also an abolitionist assisted this young man with his escape and was able to get him on board. Following the instructions from the engineer, the young man jumped from the train just before it arrived in Wilmington. Unfortunately, in doing so, he hurt his foot. The engineer had witnessed the accident and informed the others of what had occurred. A rescue party found the young man, and he was placed in a secret location where he would be hidden from the possible prying eyes of slave catchers. During this time, the Walker family, Dr. Johnson and a nurse by the name of Esther Hayes cared for the young man. After many weeks, he was well enough to leave James Walker's house.[108]

Dr. Johnson was at his office a few years later when his nurse told him that a young man wanted to speak with him. The nurse brought the man in to Dr. Johnson's office, whereupon the young man asked Dr. Johnson if he knew who he was. Dr. Johnson said he did not. It was at this point that the young man informed him he was the freedom seeker who had been at James Walker's house. He said Dr. Johnson had nursed him back to health with the help of Nurse Hayes. He had come back to thank those who were involved in his flight to freedom. He was pleased to introduce himself as Johnson Hayes Walker—no longer a number, he was a free man with a real name, a name that reflected the three kind people who helped him survive and thrive.[109]

James N. Taylor

From an early age, James N. Taylor was sympathetic to the antislavery movement. Of Taylor, it was said: "He was so nearly White that but few would have suspected that in his veins flowed a trace of African blood." He first lived in East Fallowfield, Southern Chester County, at which point, he was not involved with the Underground Railroad, but he would provide assistance to any fugitives who happened upon his home. In 1841, he moved to West Marlborough in Southern Chester County, where his reputation for helping freedom seekers grew. It was at this time that his home became a branch station on the Underground Railroad.[110]

After the Christiana Riot and being aware of Taylor's involvement with the Underground Railroad, William Parker, his brother-in-law, and another man fled to Taylor's home. Taylor transported the three men to the home of Isaac Mendenhall, located outside of Kennett Square.[111]

Thomas Fitzgerald

Thomas Fitzgerald's house and barn were located in Hinsonville and served as a station on the Underground Railroad. Freedom seekers traveling from Maryland and Virginia would pass this way as they journeyed from the Mason-Dixon line to the North. Upon arriving at Thomas's house, the freedom seekers were told they would be able to find shelter in the barn. If the freedom seekers smoked, they were requested to leave their pipe and tobacco with Thomas.[112]

Thomas would tell his visitors that they were welcome to share breakfast with him in the morning. However, if they chose to leave prior to dawn, they would find their pipe and tobacco outside the barn. Thomas's only request was the freedom seekers not burn his barn down.[113]

Harriet Walker Hood

Harriet Walker Hood was the wife of Levi Hood, a Black minister who was the pastor of the Bucktoe African Union Church. Harriet worked with members of the Longwood Progressive Friends Meeting on various abolitionist committees. She was a member of the Pennsylvania Anti-Slavery Society. Her husband knew many other Black ministers, and this afforded Harriet many opportunities to speak about abolitionism. Along with speaking at various churches, she traveled to speak at other meetings when requested.[114]

Other Black Americans

Other Black individuals who were a part of the Underground Railroad in Kennett Square included Nelson Wiggins, Reuben Wiggins, Perry Augustus, David Augustus and Joseph and Jane Wilson.[115]

Davy and Jackson were known to assist freedom seekers coming out of Wilmington, Delaware. To help fugitives reach the Mason-Dixon line and Chester County, Thomas Garrett employed a number of Black men. These men included Comegys Munson, Severn Johnson, Harry Craig and Joseph Walker.[116]

EDWIN BROSIUS, SAMUEL PENNOCK AND THE EAST LINDEN STREET HISTORIC DISTRICT KENNETT SQUARE

The rich and diverse history of East Linden Street includes Quakers, abolitionists, Underground Railroad agents, free Black people, freedom seekers, two churches and Black and White families living in harmony, side by side.

Historic East Linden Street was founded by two Quakers who were staunch abolitionists, Underground Railroad agents and successful businessmen. Their business acumen allowed both men to purchase the land that would become East Linden Street. Edwin Brosius purchased land on East Linden Street to build his home and pottery factory. Samuel Pennock and his two brothers, Jesse and Morton, bought a large amount of land on East Linden Street to build homes for themselves, as well as their employees, who worked in Pennock's agricultural machinery factory nearby.

Edwin Brosius was the son of Mahlon Brosius, who had a successful pottery business in Upper Oxford Township. It was on this farm that Edwin learned the pottery business, became an abolitionist and assisted his father with Underground Railroad activities. Edwin learned how to hide freedom seekers among the hay in the wagons he used to transport his father's pottery. So, when Edwin, at the age of twenty-one, began his pottery business in Kennett Square, he was already well versed in the art of deception when it came to transporting freedom seekers to the next station on the Underground Railroad.

Aside from his pottery business, Edwin was active in the Kennett community, serving on the borough council and the Kennett School Board. He was also the Kennett Square burgess, a director of the First National Bank of West Chester and a director of the Mutual Fire Insurance Company of Chester County.[117]

Edwin purchased land on East Linden Street to build his home and his factory. On the north side of East Linden Street, he owned parcel no. 213, where he built his first house. He later moved to 119 East Linden Street. On the south side of East Linden Street, he owned parcel nos. 200, 202, 204 and 206, where he built his pottery factory, which was located at the corner of North Broad and East Linden Streets. The factory was located there until 1885, when Edwin died. The factory was torn down, and the four parcels were purchased by Mary B. and S. Bernard Chambers, who built houses on them. Edwin also owned parcel no. 310, which was sold to Mary B. Chambers after Edwin's death in 1885.[118]

Samuel Pennock was known for being an abolitionist and an agent on the Underground Railroad. He was also known for his agricultural machinery inventions. The "iron harvester" was invented and patented by Pennock in 1859. This was the first mowing machine that had a cutter bar whose height could be adjusted by the farmer from their

East Linden Street in Kennett Square, Pennsylvania, is reported to be the oldest integrated street in the United States. It has remained integrated through present day. *Author's collection.*

tractor seat—unlike before, when the farmer would have to get off their tractor and manually adjust the cutter bar. The "Pennock road machine" was invented by Pennock in 1873; this revolutionized the construction and repair of American roads.[119]

Samuel Pennock and his two brothers, Jesse and Morton, bought a large amount of land on East Linden Street to build homes for themselves, as well as their employees. They owned on the north side of East Linden Street— parcel nos. 315, 317, 319, 323, 327, 329, 331, 333 and 335. On the south side, they owned parcel nos. 322, 324 and 328.[120] The Pennock Foundry was located on the northwest corner of State and Willow Streets.

East Linden Street is reported to be the oldest integrated street in the country. Many Underground Railroad agents lived on East Linden Street, including Vincent and Joanna Barnard, Samuel and Deborah Pennock, various members of the Cox family, Edwin Brosius and Levi Preston (Ann Preston's brother).[121]

For proof of the diversity that existed on the street, one only needs to refer to the 1860 census, which showed:

The Black Veasey family lived next door to the White Prestons. African-American blacksmith Matthew Pennywell and his family lived near White master iron worker Solomon Mercer. James and Elizabeth Walker and their children were neighbors to Thomas and Eliza Millhouse. Walker, a Black man, was a farm laborer, and his neighbor Millhouse, a White man, was a watchmaker. On one side of the home of Hannah Lamborn, a White woman, were the Black Nicholasons, and on the other, Emery and Mary Brown's family, also Black.[122]

This tradition continued with the 1910 census, which showed:

A mixed neighborhood with, for instance, former fugitive slave Joseph Carter living two doors from Edith Pennock of the Quaker abolitionist family. That same year, there was a string of Black families living on the north side—Langs, Reeds, Cramers, Millers—and then Whites: Robinsons, Prestons, Coxes, Chandlers, Grubbs.[123]

Even today, the tradition of diversity, with Black and White families living side by side in the same community, continues on East Linden Street. All of this came about because of two men and their vision to build factories, supply jobs, provide housing and treat each person with dignity and respect— whether they were White, Black or a fugitive aboard the Underground Railroad to freedom.

LOCAL UNDERGROUND STATIONS

The home of Isaac and Dinah Mendenhall was the closest station to the Delaware-Pennsylvania line. It was the first station that Thomas Garrett would instruct freedom seekers to travel to; they were to walk until they reached a stone gate, where they would go down the driveway. Built in 1840, Oakdale provided a safe haven for freedom-seeking fugitives. There were a number of places the Mendenhalls would hide fugitives. There was a spring house that was used for women and children. Men would be taken to the barn.[124] Aside from the two outbuildings, there was also a secret room that was located between a huge fireplace and a wall.[125]

John and Hannah Cox were not only staunch abolitionists, but they were also extremely active with the Underground Railroad. Their home was frequently visited by freedom seekers; they were always welcomed and offered food, clothing and shelter. The Coxes named their farm "Longwood," and John Cox later sold part of his land to build the Longwood Progressive Friends

Oakdale was a station on the Underground Railroad. There was a secret room in the house between a huge fireplace and a wall to hide freedom-seeking enslaved people. *Courtesy of the Chester County History Center.*

The barn at Oakdale was used to hide male freedom-seeking enslaved people. *Courtesy of the Chester County History Center.*

The spring house at Oakdale was used to hide women and children who were seeking freedom. *Courtesy of the Chester County History Center.*

Meetinghouse. Furthermore, Pierre du Pont used the name Longwood for the adjoining property, which he purchased in 1906. Longwood Gardens was also named after the original Longwood.[126]

The house had a widow's walk, where lookouts could be posted to watch for slave catchers. In order to keep the fugitives safe, they were hidden in the home's large attic or basement. If freedom seekers were at risk of being discovered in the house, there was a tunnel that led to the barn.[127]

OAKDALE

Oakdale is located 12.8 miles from the author's home.

It was the home of Isaac and Dinah Mendenall, who were both abolitionists, members of the Underground Railroad and founding members of the Longwood Progressive Friends Meeting.

The house had a concealed room built in between the walk-in fireplace to hide freedom seekers. There was also a fake wall that hid a room in the carriage house, where freedom seekers could be hidden. The barn was used to hide freedom-seeking males. The spring house was used to hide freedom-seeking women and children.

507 Hillendale Road
Chadds Ford, PA 19317
This house is not open to the public.

~

LONGWOOD FARM

Longwood Farm is located 9.7 miles from the author's home. It was the home of John and Hannah Cox. Their home served as a refuge for many freedom seekers. The freedom seekers were hidden in the home's large attic or in the basement. The basement had a tunnel that went to the barn, so the freedom seekers could escape slave catchers.

On the top of the house, there was a large widow's walk, which served as a lookout for slave catchers on the prowl.

735 East Baltimore Pike
Kennett Square, PA 19348
This site is currently under consideration for restoration and is not open to the public.

~

THE PINES

The Pines is located 7.4 miles from the author's home. It was the home of Dr. Bartholomew Fussell and was a safe haven for freedom seekers. A root cellar offered protection from roaming slave catchers.

Along with offering food and shelter, Dr. Fussell offered medical help to those in need.

735 East Baltimore Pike
Kennett Square, PA 1938
This home is not open to the public.

Above: Longwood Farm provided shelter in its basement and attic. There was a tunnel through which freedom-seeking enslaved people could escape. *Courtesy of the Chester County History Center.*

Left: Longwood Farm is owned by Longwood Gardens and is presently awaiting funding for its restoration. *Author's collection.*

The Pines provided a safe haven for freedom-seeking enslaved people who could hide in the root cellar. *Author's collection.*

The Pines was the home of Dr. Bartholomew Fussell and his wife—both of whom were ardent abolitionists and very active with the Underground Railroad. Thomas Garrett sent many freedom seekers to the Mendenhalls, the Coxes and the Fussells. If Thomas Garrett believed a fugitive needed immediate medical care, he would instruct them to go to Dr. Fussell. The Pines was later owned by Chandler and Hannah Darlington, who continued to maintain the property as a station on the Underground Railroad.

A root cellar was used to hide fugitives from the prying eyes of slave catchers who might be roaming the area.[128] After receiving food and shelter, the freedom seekers would be taken by a conductor to the next station of the Underground Railroad. It is estimated that, in his lifetime, Dr. Fussell and his wife assisted over two thousand slaves on their journeys to freedom.[129]

Waystations

Along with the better-known stations on the Underground Railroad in Southern Chester County, there were also waystations that were utilized. These were used when slave owners and slave catchers were too active in and around the other stations. In order to keep slave owners and slave catchers from second guessing where their bounty was hidden, freedom seekers would be brought to these way stations.[130]

The Underground Railroad consisted of people who did not believe that Black people were second-class human beings. Drawing on their moral convictions, they worked fervently to see that those people seeking freedom achieved that dream. Although the era of slavery in the United States was a terrible time, the Underground Railroad proved that there are people who are willing to follow their moral compass for the good of humanity, even if it meant putting their lives and livelihoods in danger.

KENNETT HERITAGE CENTER

The Kennett Heritage Center (KHC) also houses the Kennett Underground Railroad Center. KHC is located 7.9 miles from the author's house. There is a wealth of information available there. Volunteers are on hand to answer questions and provide walking maps if visitors want to take either a walking tour of Kennett Square or a longer driving tour that covers many sites involved with the Underground Railroad and the abolitionist movement. As its website proclaims: "The mission of the KHC is to research and document, and to celebrate Kennett's unique history."

The Kennett Heritage Center
120 North Union Street
Kennett Square, PA 19348
610-314-9313
KennettHeritageCenter@gmail.com

The Kennett Underground Railroad Center
120 North Union Street
Kennett Square, PA 19348
484-544-5070
info@kennettundergroundrr.org

THE ABOLITIONIST MOVEMENT

Timeline of the Abolitionist Movement in Pennsylvania (With Specific Events in Southern Chester County)

1711

Pennsylvania prohibits the importation of Black people and Natives.

1712

Pennsylvania prohibits the importation of enslaved people.

1775

The Pennsylvania Abolition Society is founded.

1776

In Philadelphia, Pennsylvania, the Society of Friends, whose members are also known as the Quakers, forbids its members from holding enslaved people.

1780

The Pennsylvania legislature passes an act for the gradual abolition of slavery.

1818

The American Colonization Society is formed.

1826

The Pennsylvania legislature passes an antikidnapping law to protect free Black people.

1832

In Oxford, Pennsylvania, the Oxford Clarkson Anti-Slavery Society is founded.

1833

The American Anti-Slavery Society is founded in Philadelphia.

In Oxford, Pennsylvania, the Oxford Free Produce Society is founded.

1834

The Philadelphia Anti-Slavery Society is founded.

1835

In Kennett Square, Pennsylvania, the Kennett Anti-Slavery Society is founded. John Cox is installed as its first president.

The East Fallowfield Anti-Slavery Society is founded.

1837

The Chester County Anti-Slavery Society is founded.

The Pennsylvania Anti-Slavery Society is founded.

1838

The Union Free Produce Society is founded.

The second Anti-Slavery Convention of American Women takes place in Philadelphia, Pennsylvania. Proslavery mobs riot in response.

Frederick Douglass escapes slavery and becomes active in the abolitionist cause.

1839

The American Free Produce Association is founded.

1844

Sarah Pearson opens a free produce store in Hamorton, Southern Chester County, Pennsylvania.

1845

The Free Produce Association Meeting of Philadelphia Meeting is founded.

1847

George Taylor of Kaolin, Pennsylvania, opens a free produce store in Philadelphia.

Pennsylvania passes a personal liberty law.

1849

In Unionville, Pennsylvania, the Unionville Anti-Slavery Society is founded.

The kidnapping of Thomas Mitchell in Kennett Square, Pennsylvania, strengthens the abolitionist movement.

1851

The Parker sisters' kidnapping in Southern Chester County strengthens the abolitionist movement.

1852

Uncle Tom's Cabin by Harriet Beecher Stow is published.

1853

The Longwood Progressive Friends Meetinghouse (LPFM) is founded.

1857

The *Dred Scott* decision, which states that enslaved people are not citizens but the property of their owners, is handed down. This decision further strengthens the abolitionist movement.

1860

The Pennsylvania legislature passes a liberty law outlawing use of state facilities or officials to enforce the federal Fugitive Slave Act of 1850, among other protections.

1862

Six members of the LPFM meet with President Lincoln and present him with a petition urging the widespread emancipation of enslaved people.

Weeks later, President Lincoln presents the first draft of the Emancipation Proclamation to his cabinet.

December 31, 1862

The first "watch night" is held in anticipation of President Lincoln's issue of the Emancipation Proclamation.

1863

The Emancipation Proclamation is issued by President Lincoln on January 1.

The Emancipation Proclamation is signed by President Lincoln on September 22.

The Fifty-Fourth Massachusetts Volunteer Infantry is the first all-Black regiment recruited in the North for the Union army.

Hinsonville men enlisted in the Union army, including six men in the Fifty-Fourth Massachusetts Volunteer Infantry.

The Fifty-Fourth Massachusetts Volunteer Infantry leads a heroic attack on Fort Wagner in South Carolina.

1865

The Thirteenth Amendment abolishes slavery and involuntary servitude.

1868

The Fourteenth Amendment establishes that everyone born or naturalized in the United States is a citizen.

1870

The Fifteenth Amendment affirms that the right of citizens of the United States to vote shall not be denied on account of race, color or previous condition of servitude.[131]

The abolitionist movement comprised a variety of people, programs and personalities.

In this chapter, you will learn about these various people and programs and the impact each had on the abolitionist movement. In order to educate colonists about the horrors of slavery and the need to end it, antislavery/abolitionist societies were founded. The first abolition society, the Pennsylvania Abolition Society, was founded in Pennsylvania in 1775. Some abolitionist believed the pace of gradual emancipation by following the letter of the law was too slow, so they broke off and founded the American Anti-Slavery Society, which wanted an end to slavery immediately.

A number of antislavery/abolition societies were founded in Chester County. Southern Chester County was host to the Oxford Clarkson Anti-Slavery Society, the Kennett Square Anti-Slavery Society and the Unionville Anti-Slavery Society. Most of the antislavery/abolition societies were active through the end of the Civil War, at which point, their mission was completed.

Another important and thought-provoking society was the Free Produce Society. This society was brought about by Quakers, who believed purchasing and using items produced by enslaved labor was tantamount to supporting slavery, which, in fact, they were opposed to. The various free produce stores around the Kennett Square area helped educate people about what slavery truly was.

Three events occurred that had large effects on the abolitionist movement. The first was the kidnapping of two free Black girls from Southern Chester County. The second was the kidnapping of a Black man from his Southern Chester County home in the dead of night. The third occurred just over the Chester County line in Christiana and was known as the Christiana Riot or Resistance. These three events strengthened the resolve of the abolitionist movement.

Kennett Square was synonymous with abolition. Kennett Square was actually called the "hotbed of abolition." The abolitionist movement culminated in "watch nights"—Black Americans waiting and watching with high anticipation an event that would have a lasting effect on their lives and futures.

ANTISLAVERY/ABOLITION SOCIETIES

Prior to 1775, many citizens were becoming disillusioned with the English king and desired to be free from the tyranny and oppression of the crown. At the same time, many citizens realized slavery was wrong and thought it should be ended. On April 14, 1775, a group of men met in Philadelphia and founded the Pennsylvania Abolition Society, thus beginning the struggle to combat and end slavery. On April 19, 1775, the "shot heard around the world" was fired at the Battles of Lexington and Concord in Massachusetts, marking the beginning of the American Revolution. One conflict was to end the tyranny of slavery and the other the tyranny of an oppressive king. One used weapons of war, and the other used words as weapons.

This was the beginning of antislavery and abolition societies in what was to become the United States of America. These societies employed a variety of methods for communicating their message—placing articles in newspapers and speaking at various town halls, churches and rallies. At the various meetings and rallies, pamphlets were distributed, explaining their cause. Along with publishing and speaking, members contributed time and money to helping fugitives who had crossed the Mason-Dixon line into freedom.

There were a variety of antislavery and abolitionist societies that all served the same purpose: educating the public about the horrors of slavery and the need to end the practice. However, there was a difference between the two societies: the abolitionist societies wanted gradual emancipation, and the antislavery societies wanted immediate emancipation. In Southern Chester County, these societies included the Oxford Clarkson Anti-Slavery Society, the Chester County Abolitionist Society, the Chester County Anti-Slavery Society, the Kennett Square Anti-Slavery Society and the Unionville Anti-Slavery Society.

Pennsylvania was known as the center of the American Revolution for its role in the nation's fight for independence. The Declaration of Independence was signed in Philadelphia. So, it is no surprise that the first abolitionist society was founded in Philadelphia in 1775. Originally, it was called the Pennsylvania Society for Promoting the Abolition of Slavery, for the Relief of Free Negroes Unlawfully Held in Bondage, and for Improving the Condition of the African Race. Eventually, the name was shortened to the Pennsylvania Abolition Society.[132]

Pennsylvania holds the distinction of many firsts when it comes to the abolition of slavery:

1. It was the site of the first formal protest ever made against slavery in North America.
2. It was the site of the first organized agitation against slavery.
3. It was home to the first and greatest abolitionist societies (including the Pennsylvania Abolition Society).
4. It was the first state to pass a law to bring slavery to an end.[133]

PENNSYLVANIA ABOLITION SOCIETY

The Pennsylvania Abolition Society was founded in Philadelphia on April 14, 1775. Originally, the society was known as the Society for the Relief of Free Negroes, unlawfully held in Bondage." Following the Revolutionary War, the society was renamed and called the "Pennsylvania Society for Promoting the Abolition of Slavery, for the Relief of Free Negroes Unlawfully Held in Bondage, and for Improving the Condition of the African Race."[134] Eventually, it went by the name of the Pennsylvania Abolition Society.

The Gradual Emancipation Act of 1780 had been passed by the Pennsylvania legislature, and enslaved people and free Black people began coming to Pennsylvania. Slave catchers came as well. The society wanted to assist those free Black people who were unlawfully captured and taken into bondage (hence the "relief of free negroes unlawfully held in bondage"), and society members worked tirelessly to do so. The society wanted to also help free Black people and enslaved people who came into Pennsylvania (hence "improving the condition of the African race").

Since many members were Quakers, the society chose not to use violence or civil unrest to end slavery; rather, it believed the use of "persuasion and enlightenment" would accomplish the goal of ending slavery. Furthermore, the society believed that the only way enslaved people should be freed was through the court system and other legal measures.[135] For some abolitionists, the pace of freeing the enslaved was taking too long; they became disenchanted with the slow pace and wanted immediate results. So, they founded the American Anti-Slavery Society and the Pennsylvania Anti-Slavery Society.[136]

CHESTER COUNTY ABOLITION SOCIETY

The Chester County Abolition Society's position was similar to other abolition societies, and it called for the enslaved to be emancipated gradually. This was to be accomplished by obeying the law of the land. The pace at which this society and others like it moved did not satisfy the abolitionists who wanted slavery to end immediately. In response to this frustrating position, the American Anti-Slavery Society came into existence.

AMERICAN ANTI-SLAVERY SOCIETY

The American Anti-Slavery Society was founded in Philadelphia in 1833 in response to the perceived slow pace of the Pennsylvania Abolition Society. As one of the best-known antislavery societies, its message was loud and clear: it wanted the immediate emancipation of all enslaved people. Furthermore, the society wanted the same rights granted to White people to be granted to Black people.[137]

Society speakers traveled throughout the North in an attempt to present their case that slavery was unacceptable and should be ended immediately. Frederick Douglass was not only active in the society leadership, but he was also often invited to speak on its behalf.[138]

William Lloyd Garrison, a well-known antislavery speaker, became the leader of the society. Eventually, Garrison was able to boast that the society had over 150,000 members.

The Pennsylvania Anti-Slavery Society was a part of the American Anti-Slavery Society's association.[139]

Dr. Bartholomew Fussell of Kennett Square, Pennsylvania, was a signer of the "Declaration of Sentiments" for the society, as well as a founding member. Under the auspices of the American Anti-Slavery Society, nationwide branches were formed. The first branch in Southern Chester County was the Clarkson Anti-Slavery Society.[140]

OXFORD CLARKSON ANTI-SLAVERY SOCIETY:

Dr. Bartholomew Fussell was active in the Oxford Clarkson Anti-Slavery Society, along with other abolitionists from the Southern Chester County region.[141] The preamble to the constitution of the Oxford Clarkson Anti-Slavery Society, founded 1832 in Oxford, Pennsylvania, reads as follows:

> *The practice of slavery is derogatory to the character and inconsistent with the fundamental doctrines of the republican institutions—it is alike repugnant to the principles of justice and sound policy, and to the precepts of morality and religion. Yet, unhappily for our country, this monster of iniquity has acquired such magnitude that it threatens to produce the most deplorable calamities and alleviate those evils should be a leading object with the patriot and the philanthropist.*
>
> *Knowledge is power—the most efficient power which the intellectual beings have a right to exercise on each other—to acquire and judiciously to apply this power to the extinction of slavery, requires extensive inquiry and close investigation into the nature and circumstances of the slave system. We the subscribers have therefore associated under the titles of the "The Clarkson Anti-Slavery [Society]," for the purpose of promoting useful knowledge on the subject of slavery and to use our influence for the extinction thereof.[142]*

The Clarkson Anti-Slavery Society presented a memorial to the Pennsylvania Senate and House of Representatives during its November 1840 session. In the memorial were laid out the reasons that slavery was wrong, along with the detrimental effects slavery was having on the nation. It read as follows:

> *Because of their nearness to it, slavery tends to debase the morals of the people and to produce an indifference respecting the rights of others; slavery*

leads to weakness, making the slave states a real liability in case of war; slavery leads to loss of respect by other nations towards the Unites States; it is producing a split within the Union; it works a hardship on the free people of color who may visit the South or be taken for a fugitive slave in the North.[143]

Frederick Douglass attended a meeting of the Clarkson Anti-Slavery Society on August 24, 1844. Writing to a friend about his experience at this meeting, he wrote:

This society is very appropriately named; it is certainly one of the most venerable and impressive antislavery bodies with which it has been my fortune to meet....The attendance at the meeting was very large; many had to stand outside, not being able to gain admission into the house. The society got through their business at an early hour, to give place to addresses of Friend Redmond and myself upon the general subject of slavery and antislavery. Our remarks were listened to, both within and without the house, with a deep stillness that indicated an absorbing interest in the subjects we were but feebly attempting to set forth.[144]

The last recorded meeting of the Oxford Clarkson Anti-Slavery Society was held on August 28, 1849. The meeting took place at the Hosanna Meeting House, next to Hinsonville, Pennsylvania.

PENNSYLVANIA ANTI-SLAVERY SOCIETY

The Pennsylvania Anti-Slavery Society was founded in 1837. Dr. Bartholomew Fussell of Kennett Square was elected to the position of vice-president. The annual meetings of the society were held in Kennett Square. At one such meeting, the following resolutions were adopted:

The Constitution was condemned for "helping to sustain the unrighteous system" of slavery; because such is "contrary to the law of God" that part of the Constitution should not be obeyed; voting under or swearing to uphold the Constitution makes one a party to it; and antislavery people should not take office or vote under the Constitution so long as such "pro-slavery features remain."[145]

The Pennsylvania Anti-Slavery Society continued meeting throughout the Civil War. It began with the call for the immediate end to slavery, and that was continued throughout its existence.

CHESTER COUNTY ANTI-SLAVERY SOCIETY

The Chester County Anti-Slavery Society was a branch of the American Anti-Slavery Society. An advertisement was placed in the *West Chester Register and Examiner* on February 28, 1837, which read:

> *The friends of the abolition of slavery in the United States, residing in Chester County, are requested to meet in convention, at the courthouse, in West Chester, on the fourth day of March next, at 10 o'clock in the morning, for the purpose of conferring together on the subject of forming a county antislavery society. The convention will be addressed by C.C. Burleigh and other friends of the cause of abolition. It is confidently hoped that the convention will be large—that every friend of the oppressed will give his attendance on this occasion, unless rendered unable by some providential circumstance.*
>
> *—Many Friends of the Cause*[146]

The *Coatesville Weekly Times*, on November 21, 1837, reported:

> *The Chester County Anti-Slavery Society will hold its first annual meeting in Coatesville, on third day, (Tuesday) the 28th of next month, commencing at 10 o'clock AM. It is very desirable that every society in the county should be duly represented, as it is anticipated subjects of great interest will be before the meeting for its action....Our friends and public, generally, are earnestly and respectfully invited to attend.*[147]

Membership in the Chester County Anti-Slavery Society was drawn from members of other antislavery groups in Chester County. At their meeting following the passage of the Fugitive Slave Act of 1850, the society refused to back the act. Members felt it was necessary to obey what they called the "higher law" instead of a man-made law that encouraged the continued enslavement of other human beings as well as the kidnapping of free Black people to be brought back South and enslaved as well.[148]

KENNETT SQUARE ANTI-SLAVERY SOCIETY

The Quakers in Chester County were involved in the abolitionist movement. Founded in 1835, the Kennett Square Anti-Slavery Society was a branch of the American Anti-Slavery Society. John Cox, an abolitionist and stationmaster of the Underground Railroad, was the first president of the society. Along with the goal of immediately emancipating the enslaved, in 1838, the society stated that any person who "aids in the restoration of the fugitive to his master is guilty of a crime against humanity and religion."[149]

James N. Taylor transported William Parker, Parker's brother-in-law, and another fugitive from his home to the Mendenhalls' house after the Christiana Riot. Taylor helped found the Kennett Square Anti-Slavery Society.[150]

EAST FALLOWFIELD ANTI-SLAVERY SOCIETY

The East Fallowfield Anti-Slavery Society was founded in 1835. The society held its meetings in the Fallowfield Meetinghouse until 1845. This is when the East Fallowfield Riot occurred, after which the society was banned from holding any further meetings at the meetinghouse. The meetinghouse membership voted for the ban.[151] In response to being banned from meeting at the Fallowfield Quaker Meeting, members of the society banned together and built the People's Hall in 1845 for their society meetings. People's Hall is located just a short distance from the Fallowfield Meetinghouse.

East Fallowfield Meetinghouse was the site of the "East Fallowfield Riot," after which the East Fallowfield Anti-Slavery Society was banned from the meetinghouse. *Author's collection.*

UNIONVILLE ANTI-SLAVERY SOCIETY

The Unionville Anti-Slavery Society was a branch of the American Anti-Slavery Society, and its members were Black. This society was formed in 1849 with the mission of educating Black people about the importance of the antislavery movement. With the recent passage of the Fugitive Slave Act of 1850, the leadership of the Unionville Anti-Slavery Society hoped to explain what this new act meant to Black people.[152]

In the October 3, 1850 issue of the *Pennsylvania Freeman*, it was reported that the Chester County Anti-Slavery Society held its annual meeting on Saturday, September 21. At this meeting, James Walker, who was active in the Underground Railroad movement in Kennett Square, reported:

> [The Unionville Anti-Slavery Society] *was still in existence and had held several meetings; but that it had met with unexpected opposition from colored people themselves, and less encouragement than they had hoped from their white brethren, to whom they had looked for aid, counsel, and sympathy in their meetings....But notwithstanding their discouragements, the members of the society were resolved to persevere and do what they could.*
>
> *Thomas Whitson expressed his gratification at this resolution of perseverance in antislavery work....He hoped this movement among our colored friends would be encourage by the attendance of abolitionists generally at their meetings, and by such sympathy and counsel as we could give, and he believed that such an intercourse and union of effort would prove mutually beneficial. Amos Preston* [Ann Preston's father] *and others joined in similar expressions of sympathy, and desire for a more general interest in the meetings of the Unionville society.*[153]

FREE PRODUCE MOVEMENT

Quakers did not approve of certain activities, which they believed brought dishonor to their society. This was especially true of the questionable activities utilized to obtain money, such as gambling.[154] The Amish denounced and condemned members for reprobate behavior, and Quakers did likewise. After the Quakers banned members from owning enslaved people, the Quakers realized owning products produced by enslaved people was the equivalent of owning enslaved people. Thus, the free produce movement was started as a way to educate members and others about the evils of slavery and the importance of not purchasing slave-produced products.

The free produce movement not only educated people about how wrong slavery was, but it also wanted to help people understand that consuming slave-produced products supported slavery and the slave owners who profited from their enslaved people. The free produce movement was one form of abolitionism—if you stopped purchasing slave-produced products, you created economic harm for slave owners.

There were a number of free produce societies that formed in the early 1800s. In the 1820s, the Wilmington Society for the Encouragement of Free Labor and the Pennsylvania Free Produce Societies helped found the American Free Produce Association in 1839. Then in 1845, the Quakers founded the Free Produce Association Meeting of Philadelphia Meeting.[155] Around 1838, the Free Produce Association of Chester County was founded.[156] In 1833, the Oxford Free Produce Society was founded.[157]

George Taylor of Kaolin, Pennsylvania, opened a free produce store in Philadelphia.[158] George Taylor leased the Rosenvich Mill to produce cotton. The mill was located on the Doe Run, near Cochranville, Pennsylvania, in order to have waterpower. The mill was in operation from 1854 to 1858, when, due to the depression of 1857, it was no longer economically feasible for it to remain in operation.[159] In 1844, Sarah Pearson opened a free produce store in Hamorton, Pennsylvania. The store ran from 1844 to 1858.[160]

The free produce movement was thought by both Black and White to be an honorable endeavor; however, it never gained traction among abolitionists. It did not have the appeal that writing congressmen, holding antislavery rallies and assisting with the Underground Railroad did. People were looking for more immediate results, and buying non-slave-produced products did not have that result. The hope that boycotting slave-produced products would harm slave owners and help the enslaved never came to fruition. Furthermore, non-slave-produced products were often of an inferior quality. Trying to obtain raw materials to produce goods proved challenging as well—they could be difficult to obtain and, at times, hard to certify that they were not produced by enslaved people. Due to disappointing results and a lack of support, the movement ceased to exist.

PARKER SISTER
KIDNAPPINGS

East Nottingham, where Elizabeth Parker was kidnapped, is 10.9 miles from the author's home. West Nottingham, where Rachel Parker was kidnapped, is 15.5 miles from the author's home.

The Fugitive Slave Act of 1850 encouraged slave catchers from the South to venture north and kidnap Black people, whether they were free or fugitives. The kidnapping of the Parker sisters is one example of this type of activity.

Matthew Donnely of East Nottingham employed a sixteen-year-old free Black girl by the name of Elizabeth Parker. Thomas McCreary grew up in Chester County and had a reputation of being a kidnapper. In mid-December 1851, Thomas lived up to his reputation and kidnapped Elizabeth from her home and took her to the slave pens in Baltimore, Maryland, where she was sold for $1,900 and shipped to New Orleans.[161]

Just two weeks later, McCreary showed up at the house where Elizabeth's sister, Rachel, worked. Rachel, who was fifteen years old and also free, was employed by Joseph Miller. She had been under his employ for six years. When Miller answered the door, McCreary told him he needed directions. Once inside the house, McCreary grabbed Rachel, took her outside and put her in the carriage, where his fellow kidnapper was waiting. Attempting to rescue Rachel, Miller ran outside, where he was pushed away from the carriage and knocked down.[162]

Joseph Miller, along with a band of men, knew to go to the slave pen in Baltimore, where they found Rachel. Miller arranged for Rachel to be moved from the slave pen to a jail, where she would have to wait for a trial. Quakers intervened on behalf of both sisters. First, a petition for freedom was filed for Rachel. Second, a group of Quakers paid $1,500 to the New Orleans master so Elizabeth could be set free.[163]

The kidnapping of the Parker sisters furthered the cause of the abolitionist movement. *Courtesy of the Pennsylvania Historic and Museum.*

The sisters' trial was held in Baltimore, and since it was successful, the girls could return to Pennsylvania. Reverend John Miller Dickey, one of the cofounders of the Ashmun Institute, along with other concerned citizens, raised $1,000 to help pay for the trial. Joseph Miller, Rachel's employer, was murdered on his way back from Baltimore, which caused a huge public outcry. Pennsylvania leaders responded to this outcry and paid out $3,000 toward the trial.[164]

Sentiment was already running against the Fugitive Slave Act of 1850. The kidnapping of two free Black girls further illuminated the injustice of this law, as well as the injustice of slavery itself. Although there had been other kidnappings of free Black people and fugitives, the kidnapping of the Parker sisters furthered the cause of the abolitionist movement.

Taggart's Crossroads, Pennsylvania, in Southern Chester County was a small, peaceful town in 1849. That was, until August 22, when slave catchers burst into the home of Thomas Mitchell and kidnapped him. Neither Thomas's wife nor his neighbors knew Thomas was a fugitive, having escaped from his Maryland slave owner some years before. Thomas's employer was a Quaker by the name of George Martin.[165]

George Martin was familiar with the slave pens of Baltimore and headed there. Samuel Pennock, an ardent abolitionist and member of the Underground Railroad, accompanied George to Baltimore. George found the slave trader Jonathan Wilson, who was holding Mitchel. Wilson told George Martin that in order for Mitchell to be released, a sum of $600 needed to be paid. George Martin, with the help of neighbors, raised the money, so Thomas Mitchell was set free and returned to his family in Pennsylvania.[166]

> ### THOMAS MITCHELL KIDNAPPING
>
> Taggart's Crossroads, Pennsylvania (now called Willowdale), is 8.2 miles from the author's home. It was there, on August 22, 1849, that slave catchers burst into Thomas Mitchell's home in the middle of the night and kidnapped him. This event further strengthened the cause of the abolitionist movement.

In response to the kidnapping of Thomas Mitchell, the *Pennsylvania Freeman* advertised a meeting to discuss the event:

Indignation Meeting—Grand Rally!! The citizens of Chester County, without distinction of party, are required to assemble in a grand mass meeting at the house from which William [sic] Mitchell was recently kidnapped, near Taggart's Cross Roads, in East Marlborough Township, on Saturday 22nd, at 10 o'clock AM, to express their sentiments concerning that highhanded outrage, and take measure to prevent future incursions of Maryland land pirates upon them. The meeting will be held in the woods near the house if the day be fair; if not, in the barn nearby. It will continue through the afternoon. Let every person who would protect the rights of the poor, the peace of the country, the honor of the state, and his own liberties, from the midnight invasion of burglars, assassins and kidnappers, come up to this gathering of people. Speakers from abroad are expected.[167]

THE CHRISTIANA RIOT

The site of William Parker's home, where the Christiana Riot took place, is thirteen miles from the author's home. Three freedom seekers had taken refuge in William Parker's home when they learned that their owner was on the way to capture them.

The slave owner and his men did not back down, the mob that had formed to protect the freedom seekers did not back down and violence erupted, ending with the death of the slave owner.

William Parker; his brother-in-law, Alexander Pinkney; and freedom seeker Abraham Johnson fled to James N. Taylor's home. Taylor transported them to Isaac Mendenhall's home near Kennett Square. From there, they went along the Underground Railroad, where they ended in Rochester, New York. There, they were escorted by Frederick Douglass to a ship, which took them to Toronto, Canada.

Thomas Mitchell remained in Unionville with his family, which grew from having two children to ten. In 1878, Mitchell and his wife purchased a five-acre parcel of land, which included a house from the Swayne sisters, who were Quakers. Mitchell worked hard, and at the time of his death, "he owned a small parcel of land, a modestly furnished two-story house, two cows, and two pigs."[168] Mitchell had been an enslaved man, a freedom seeker and then a freed Black man. When his freedom was purchased from the slave trader Jonathan Wilson, he entered that special group of Black people who were enslaved but were then free.

The kidnapping of Thomas Mitchell was another event that furthered the cause of the abolitionist movement. Citizens were becoming more and more upset with the continued invasion of slave catchers from the South into their land.

On September 11, 1777, the Battle of the Brandywine took place. This was one of many battles that occurred during the Revolutionary War. Freedom from the tyranny of the British Crown was what was at stake in this war. Seventy-four years later, another event occurred that also represented freedom from oppression and unjust treatment.

On September 11, 1851, the Christiana Riot or Resistance took place. There, Black people defended their desire to be free from the oppressive laws and cruel treatment that they had endured under slavery.

On September 11, 2001, 150 years after the Christiana Riot, the worst attack on American soil took place.

Edward Gorsuch was a tobacco plantation owner in Maryland who owned enslaved people who carried out the work on the plantation. In 1849, four of his enslaved people escaped and headed north.

The Fugitive Slave Act of 1850 empowered slave owners and slave catchers to head north to reclaim their freedom seekers. The 1850 act mandated stiff penalties for anyone who aided and abetted freedom seekers and denied fugitives a fair trial, all of which meant slave owners and slave catchers could do almost anything they wanted to do. Then in 1851, Gorsuch got word that at two or three of his escaped enslaved people had been located at the home of a Black farmer, William Parker, who lived near Christiana, Pennsylvania.[169]

After securing warrants for the arrest of his freedom seekers, Gorsuch and a small band of men headed for William Parker's house in Christiana. Accompanying Gorsuch were his son and a deputy marshal. William Parker, a freedom seeker himself, had been teaching self-defense to other Black people in the area. There was an early warning system in place to call neighbors to come help when necessary. When Parker saw Gorsuch and his group outside his house, his wife opened a second-story window and blew a horn as a call for help. Responding to the alarm, a number of Black residents, armed with a variety of weapons, quickly arrived at Parker's home.[170]

William Parker's White neighbor Castner Hanway was one of the first people to arrive. Seeing the tensions rising between his Black neighbors and Gorsuch, Hanway tried to reason with the two groups and have them disperse, with no avail. Both sides refused the wise counsel, and that is when gunfire erupted and Gorsuch was killed.[171]

From an early age, James N. Taylor was sympathetic to the antislavery movement. He first lived in East Fallowfield, Southern Chester County; at this point, he was not involved with the Underground Railroad but would provide assistance to any fugitives who happened upon his home. In 1841, he moved to West Marlborough in Southern Chester County, where his reputation for helping freedom seekers grew. At this time, his home became a branch station on the Underground Railroad. Aware of Taylor's willingness to assist freedom seekers, William Parker; his brother-in-law, Alexander Pinkney; and fugitive slave Abraham Johnson fled to Taylor's home.[172]

According to Graceanna Lewis, Dr. Bartholomew Fussell's niece:

Parker, Pinckney, and Johnson were taken by James N. Taylor to the home of Isaac Mendenhall, not very far from the village of Hamorton. They slept in his barn by night, husking corn in the fields by day, as if employed for that purpose, to allow the hunt for them to go by. One day, a messenger came to warn them of danger, and they fled to the woods. Isaac Mendenhall [was] intending to take them to John Vickers, near Lionville. Hearing of the alarm, my uncle Fussell visited his friend, Mendenhall, and with characteristic concern for the welfare of others, said, "Isaac, I am better acquainted with the route than thee is, and besides, I have no property to sacrifice if I am detected, and thee has. Thee start with them on the road, and I will meet thee and go on with them, and thee can return."

In accordance with this plan, he drove, not to John Vickers, but six miles farther, to our house, arriving there about midnight. He was no doubt influenced in this course by that John Vicker's house was less private than ours, and by the possibility that he might have men employed in his business whom would not be safe to trust.

Before the men were brought in, our uncle fully explained the dangerous nature of the case involving, as it did, not only the ordinary risks of harboring fugitives but of placing ourselves in antagonism to the United States government.

After assuring us of the need of the extremist caution, the men were brought into the house, and, I think, my uncle immediately returned home. The men were instructed to bolt themselves into their room until arrangements could be made for their departure. They were speedily accomplished, and before day dawned [the men] were moved out through an orchard at the back of the house to a conveyance which stood in waiting on a less-frequented road than usually taken. In the vehicle, they were covered as though they had been a load of marketing and were thus sent onward one stage of their journey to Canada.[173]

Dinah Mendenhall knew that taking the men could result in severe punishment, per the Fugitive Slave Act of 1850, but she and her husband had a firm conviction that they "would never submit to carry out that accursed Fugitive Slave Law, come what might." Even though she was scared at times, she said she "held to [her] faith in an overruling providence, and [they] came through it safely."[174]

With the help of the Underground Railroad network, William Parker, his brother-in-law, and the freedom seeker made it to "Rochester, New York, where Frederick Douglass personally escorted them to a boat bound for Canada."[175] As way of saying thanks for all Douglass had done for the three men, Parker gave Douglass the revolver that had once belonged to Gorsuch.[176]

In response to the killing of Gorsuch, anyone who was presumed to be involved with the riot was arrested. Thirty-eight men and women, black and white, were indicted on charges of treason. When Frederick Douglass heard that these men and women had been charged with treason, he was furious and said this:

This is to cap the climax of American absurdity, to say nothing of American infamy. Our government has virtually made every colored man in the land an outlaw; one who may be hunted by any villain who may think proper to do so, and if the hunted man, finding himself stripped of all legal protection, shall lift his arm in his own defense, why forsooth, he is arrested, arraigned, and tried for high treason, and if found guilty, he must suffer death. The basis of allegiance is protection. We owe allegiance to the government that protects us, but to the government that destroys us, we owe no allegiance.[177]

Castner Hanway, who had come over to the Parker place to try to calm the situation down, was arrested and accused of being "the mastermind of the riot"; he was also accused of treason, because the claim was that Hanway wanted "to levy war" against America.[178]

The trial for Hanway commenced on November 24, 1851. The defense team consisted of Thaddeus Stevens and three other lawyers. One of those lawyers was Joseph Lewis, a staunch advocate of the antislavery movement from Kennett Square. Once the trial ended, it took the jury only fifteen minutes to return a not guilty verdict.[179]

In the aftermath of the Christiana Riot and trial of Castner Hanway, the abolitionist movement gained strength, and others joined the cause, including Hanway himself.[180]

Although the Fugitive Slave Act of 1850 took rights away from Black Americans, the Christiana Riot showed them that they could defend themselves and resist oppression and slave catchers alike.

During October 1850, members of the Chester County Anti-Slavery Society united in their opposition to the Fugitive Slave Act of 1850. Members believed they had to "obey the higher law," which saw created beings as equal, rather than a man-made law, which did not. At its meeting the next year, the Chester County Anti-Slavery Society defended the Christiana Riot by stating it was "the legitimate fruit, primarily, of the system of American slavery… and the Fugitive Slave Law, which virtually wages a man-hunting war upon the communities of the North."[181] William Parker stated, "Human rights are mutual and reciprocal. If you take my liberty and life, you forfeit your own."[182]

When asked about assisting the three men, Douglass responded, "I could not look upon them as murderers. To me, they were heroic defenders of the just right of man against man stealers and murderers. So, I fed them and sheltered them in my house."[183]

Furthermore, Frederick Douglass felt:

> *The Christiana Conflict was…needed to check* [the aggressions of slave catchers] *and to bring the hunters of men to the sober second thought…. If it be right for any man to resist those who would enslave them, it was right for the men of color at Christiana to resist….Life and liberty are the most sacred of all man's rights….The man who rushes out of the orbit of his own rights to strike down the rights of another does, by that act, divest himself of the right to live, if he be shot down, the punishment is just. The Christiana Resisters were justified and righteous in taking their stand.*[184]

To mark the one hundredth anniversary of the Christiana Riot, an event was held in Christiana. One of the speakers was Dr. Horace Mann Bond, the then-president of Lincoln University. Dr. Bond thanked

The Christiana Riot showed Black people that they could defend themselves and resist oppressors and slavecatchers alike. *Courtesy of the Pennsylvania Historic and Museum.*

Thaddeus Stevens, as a Pennsylvania legislator who made sure a bill was passed to grant Ashmun Institute a charter to open in 1854. Ashmun later was renamed Lincoln University in honor of President Lincoln, who had recently been assassinated.[185]

Dr. Bond went on to say he wanted to "speak principally of the man who… seems to me to be the symbol—the distilled essence—of the meaning of the Christiana Riot.…His name was William Parker.…This is the centennial of the violence engendered by great passions and forces, but also by one man." William Parker, according to Bond, was "a man who loved freedom passionately and who used violence to get it for himself and for others."[186]

Dr. Bond ended his speech with a powerful statement: "Give men freedom in this world and equality before their creator in life and in death; give men the equal protection of all the laws…everywhere in the world…[and] we shall have peace…brotherhood…love…and no Christiana Riots nor its multiplication in war's violence."[187]

KENNETT SQUARE, PENNSYLVANIA

Kennett Square, Pennsylvania, was known as the "hotbed of abolition" from the 1830s until the 1860s.[188] Kennett Square was a short distance from the Delaware-Pennsylvania border. That meant freedom seekers escaping the slave states of Delaware, Maryland, and Virginia headed for that border. The Kennett Square area had many Quakers living there. Many of them were against slavery and were abolitionists as well.

Being so close to the border meant slave owners and slave catchers would cross the border in search of their freedom seekers or free blacks who could be kidnapped and sold into slavery. These practices were unacceptable to many who lived in the Kennett area and whites and blacks joined together to oppose these activities and assist freedom seekers on their journey to freedom and away from the tyranny and oppression of their owners.

The Fugitive Slave Act of 1850 was meant to punish those who came to the aid of freedom seekers. Instead of halting the practice of providing assistance to freedom seekers, it actually strengthened the resolve of the abolitionists to do more work. In doing so, Kennett Square did indeed become "a hotbed of abolitionist activity."[189]

Kennett Square often hosted the meetings of the Pennsylvania Anti-Slavery Society. The Kennett Square Anti-Slavery Society was founded in 1835. Sarah Pearson's Free Produce Store was located just outside of

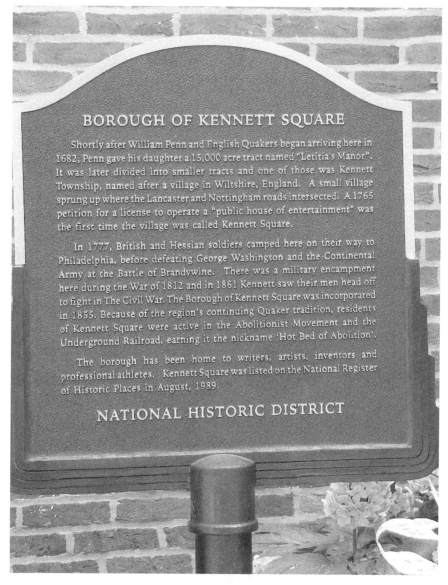

Kennett Square, Pennsylvania, was known as the hotbed of abolition and had more Underground Railroad stations in the Kennett area than any where else. *Author's collection.*

Kennett Square. Kennett Square hosted a variety of abolitionist activities and many prominent abolitionists lived in the area risking their lives, resources, and reputations to assist the freedom seekers. These people were willing to put others first.

WATCH NIGHT

Frederick Douglass, when asked what December 31, 1862, mean to him, he said it "was a day for poetry and song, a new song. These cloudless skies, this balmy air, this brilliant sunshine, (making December as pleasant as May), are in harmony with the glorious morning of liberty about to dawn up on us."[190]

What was Frederick Douglass writing about? President Abraham Lincoln promised he would be issuing a proclamation that would set the enslaved free who lived in the rebellious states. Black Americans thought this would happen on January 1, 1863, and therefore held an all-night vigil on December 31, 1862. Black people in the North held their vigils in their churches; in the South, Black people secretly gathered around "praying trees." This is how the tradition of "watch night" began.[191]

When President Abraham Lincoln signed the Emancipation Proclamation, he told those gathered with him to witness this historic event: "I never, in my life, felt more certain that I was doing right than I do in signing this paper."[192] Furthermore, Lincoln stated the Emancipation Proclamation was "the central act of my administration and the great event of the nineteenth century."[193]

Invoking his presidential authority, President Abraham Lincoln proclaimed:[194]

Whereas, on the twenty-second day of September, in the year of the Lord one thousand eight hundred and sixty-two, a proclamation was issued by the president of the United States, containing, among other things, the following to wit:

That on the first day of January, in the year of our Lord one thousand eight hundred and sixty-three, all persons held as slaves within any state or designated part of a state, the people whereof shall then be in rebellion against the Unites States, shall be then, thenceforward, and forever free; and the executive government of the United States, including the military and naval authority thereof, will recognize and maintain the freedom of such persons, and will do no act or acts to repress such persons, or any of them, in any efforts they may make for their actual freedom.

That the executive will, on the first day of January aforesaid, by proclamation, designate the states and parts of states, if any, in which the people thereof, respectively, shall then be in rebellion against the United States; and the fact that any state, or people thereof, shall on that day be, in good faith, represented in the Congress of the United States by members chosen thereof at elections wherein a majority of qualified voters of such state shall have participated, shall, in the absence of strong countervailing testimony, be deemed conclusive evidence that such state, and the people thereof, are not then in rebellion against the United States.

Now, therefore, I, Abraham Lincoln, president of the United States, by virtue of the power in me vested as commander-in-chief, of the army and navy of the United States in time of actual armed rebellion against the authority and government of the United States, and as a fit and necessary war measure for suppressing said rebellion, do, on this first day of January, in the year of our Lord one thousand eight hundred and sixty-three, and in accordance with my purpose so to do publicly proclaim for the full period of one hundred days, from the day first above mentioned, order and designate as the states and parts of states wherein the people thereof respectively, are this day in rebellion against the United States, the following, to wit: Arkansas, Texas, Louisiana, (except the Parishes of St. Bernard, Plaquemines, Jefferson, St. John, St. Charles, St. James Ascension, Assumption, Terrebonne, Lafourche, St. Mary, St. Martin, and Orleans, including the city of New Orleans) Mississippi, Alabama, Florida, Georgia, South Carolina, North Carolina, and Virginia (except the forty-eight counties designated as West Virginia, and also the counties of Berkley, Accomac, Northampton, Elizabeth City, York, Princess Ann, and Norfolk, including the cities of Norfolk and Portsmouth), and which excepted parts for the present, left precisely as if this proclamation were not issued.

And by virtue of the power, and for the purpose aforesaid, I do order and declare that all persons held as slaves within said designated states, and parts of states, are, and henceforward shall be free; and that the executive government of the United States, including the military and naval authorities thereof, will recognize and maintain the freedom of said persons.

And I hereby enjoin upon the people so declared to be free to abstain from all violence, unless in necessary self-defence [sic]; and I recommend to them that, in all cases when allowed, they labor faithfully for reasonable wages.

And I further declare and make known, that such persons of suitable condition, will be received into the armed service of the United States to garrison forts, positions, stations, and other places, and to man vessels of all sorts in said service.

And upon this act, sincerely believed to be an act of justice, warranted by the Constitution, upon military necessarily, I invoke the considerate judgment of mankind, and the gracious favor of Almighty God.

In witness thereof, I have hereunto set my hand and caused the seal of the United States to be affixed.

Done at the city of Washington, this first day of January, in the year of our Lord one thousand eight hundred and sixty three, and of the independence of the United States of America the eighty-seventh.

By the president: Abraham Lincoln
William H. Seward, secretary of state

While the Emancipation Proclamation only freed the enslaved in the Southern states that were fighting against the states of the Union, it began the fulfillment of the abolitionist movement's goal—the end of slavery all together. Following the Emancipation Proclamation, many slave states revised their state constitutions banning slavery. These included states like Maryland, which had played such a major role in the work of the Underground Railroad.

President Lincoln supported a new constitutional amendment that would officially outlaw slavery. First, the Senate passed the bill, followed by the House. Then on December 18, 1865, the Thirteenth Amendment became official. The Civil War had ended, the Thirteenth Amendment was law and slavery was abolished in the United States. The work of abolitionists was complete, and they could rejoice and declare, "The colored people by law, now have equal privileges with the White man...[although] much need[ed] to be done before they can fully enjoy the rights of United States citizenship."[195] It only took three more years before the Fourteenth Amendment became law, granting citizenship to all people born in the United States or foreigners who were naturalized.

❧ ❧ ❧

Kennett Square was home to many of these abolitionists who rejoiced over the signing of the Emancipation Proclamation and the passage of the Thirteenth Amendment. These abolitionists included such people as Isaac and Dinah Mendenhall, John and Hannah Cox, Eusebius and Sarah Barnard, Moses and Mary Pennock, Thomas Garrett and Dr. Bartholomew Fussell and his wife, Lydia. Not only were they staunch abolitionists, but they were also founding members of the Longwood Progressive Friends Meeting.

4

LONGWOOD PROGRESSIVE FRIENDS MEETING

A series of events occurred that led to the founding of the Longwood Progressive Friends Meeting (LPFM). These events involved disagreements among Quakers on how slavery should be viewed and addressed. Many of the local abolitionists and Underground Railroad stationmasters were founding members. LPFM hosted many famous speakers, including Frederick Douglass, Susan B. Anthony, Thomas Garrett and Harriet Beecher Stowe. Members of LPFM met with President Abraham Lincoln to stress the importance of emancipating the enslaved.

LPFM helped bring about the Reconstruction amendments. Because of LPFM's rich history, the National Park Service designated LPFM as a historic site. Directly across from the meeting building is the meeting cemetery, where some of the founders of LPFM are buried.

~

LONGWOOD PROGRESSIVE FRIENDS MEETING

The Longwood Progressive Friends Meetinghouse is 9.9 miles from the author's home. This meeting was founded by Quaker abolitionists who firmly believed that slavery should be ended. The issue of slavery became a point of division between conservative Quakers and progressive Quakers. Both parties believed slavery was wrong. The main disagreement was whether Quakers should embrace antislavery activity and, if so, what that would look like.

After a series of events, the progressive Quakers reached the decision that they should found their own meeting. So, in 1853, fifty-eight men and women came together to found their own meeting. Most of these founders lived in and around Kennett Square, Pennsylvania. These men and women included the Mendenhalls, Coxes, Barnards, Pennocks and Fussells.

The Meetinghouse is now home to the Brandywine Valley Tourism Information Center:

300 Greenwood Road
Kennett Square, PA 19348
484-770-8550

There is an informative display about the Underground Railroad that includes information on stationmasters, agents, conductors and the stations that were found in and around Kennett Square.

~

Timeline of Events Leading Up to the Founding of the Longwood Progressive Friends Meeting

1837

The Philadelphia Yearly Meeting instructs members "to embrace every right opportunity to maintain and exalt our religious testimony against slavery."

Progressive Quakers begin joining antislavery societies.

Progressive Quakers begin inviting paid speakers to come to Quaker meetings to lecture about slavery and the abolitionist movement.

1838

Quakers were told they should not be an "accessory to this enormous national evil [slavery], but to discourage it by all the justifiable means in their power."

For progressive Quakers, "justifiable means" equated to joining antislavery societies and assisting fugitives.

1840

Conservative friends thought Quaker perfectionism meant being a people who were "withdrawn and guarded from the world." Progressive friends believed "Quaker heritage required active involvement in efforts to reform the world."

Jesse Kersey, a prominent Chester County Quaker, objected to having non-Quakers speaking in the meeting.

Progressive Quakers believed every friend should seek every chance to speak against slavery and take an active role in opposing slavery and assisting fugitives.

1844

Progressive, antislavery Quakers became frustrated with the Society of Friends and its focus on Quaker traditions, such as dress and speech, rather than the issue of slavery. The progressives believed this made the society appear proslavery.

1845

The East Fallowfield Riot takes place. Progressive Dr. Edwin Fussell attempted to speak and was met with resistance.

The East Fallowfield Anti-Slavery Society had held its meetings in the Fallowfield Meetinghouse since the society was founded in 1835. After the East Fallowfield Riot at the Fallowfield Meetinghouse, the Quaker meeting membership banned the society from using the meetinghouse.

After being banned from the Fallowfield Meetinghouse, progressive Quakers built People's Hall for holding their own meetings.

1850

A meeting is held at the London Grove Meeting to discuss "the trouble stated of Kennett Monthly Meeting."

1851

An "unauthorized meeting" is held at the Kennett Meeting. Because of his "disorderly conduct in having associated with others in holding a meeting out of order and in subversion of the discipline of the society," William Barnard is disowned in November.

1852

Six more members of the Kennett Meeting are disowned.

Two reports from the Western Quarterly Meeting are submitted to the Philadelphia Yearly Meeting. The Conservative Report is accepted, but the Progressive Report is rejected.

The progressives submit a list of grievances to the Philadelphia Yearly Meeting in the hopes of getting some resolution to the disagreements between the conservative and progressive parties. Unfortunately, the report is refused.

The Marlborough Riot takes place June 6. Oliver Johnson, a supporter of the progressive Quakers, is arrested while trying to speak during a meeting.

In October, the decision is made to prepare a call for a General Religious Conference to be held the following year.

1853

On May 22, the call is held at the Old Kennett Meeting House.

The Pennsylvania Yearly Meeting of Progressive Friends is founded.

1854

The Longwood Progressive Friends Meeting is denied further use of the Old Kennett Meeting House.

The progressives, having held the first day of their annual meeting at Old Kennett, move to Hamorton Hall to complete their annual meeting.

1855

On May 19, the new Longwood Progressive Friends Meetinghouse is dedicated.

1940

The Longwood Progressive Friends Meeting is discontinued, and Pierre du Pont purchases the property.

Present Day

The meetinghouse is leased to Chester County Conference and Visitors Bureau, where the Brandywine Valley Tourism Information Center is located.

The meetinghouse is placed in the National Register of Historic Places.

The meetinghouse is designated a National Park Service Network to Freedom Site.

The meetinghouse is a designated stop on the Harriett Tubman Underground Railroad Byway.

The Founding of Longwood Progressive Friends Meeting

The Longwood Progressive Friends Meeting (LPFM) came into existence due to how Quakers viewed the issue of slavery. Virtually all Quakers believed the institution of slavery was wrong and should not exist. However, how that belief was put into practice created a fissure between conservative Quakers and progressive Quakers. Conservative Quakers believed simply not owning enslaved people was enough and they need not do anything else. Progressive Quakers believed assistance must be given to freedom seekers in the form of the Underground Railroad and the promotion of the emancipation of the enslaved.

During the 1837 Philadelphia Yearly Meeting, members were exhorted "to embrace every right opportunity to maintain and exalt our religious testimony against slavery.... The problem was that friends did not agree what constituted 'right openings.'" In 1881, an article in the *West Chester Daily Local News* reported:

> *Many years ago...*[Lucretia Mott] *addressed a number of friends' meetings in the townships of Marlborough, Kennett, Londongrove* [sic] *and others. The chief purpose of her discourses appeared to be a desire to arouse...a livelier appreciation of duty in connection with their religious profession respecting the anti-slavery cause—urging that the open, active affiliation with abolitionists and their society, was an important part of their obligations as professing Christians.*
>
> *At the time, a considerable number of prominent friends earnestly opposed active cooperation and union with anti-slavery associations, believing that a*

The Longwood Progressive Friends Meetinghouse was home to Quaker abolitionists who believed actions not words were needed to end slavery. *Courtesy of the Chester County History Center.*

consistent adherence to their testimonies as a religious body was all that was required of them in relation to the practice of slaveholding.[196]

The Kennett Square Anti-Slavery Society was very active, even before LPFM came into existence. On May 12, 1838, the society issued a "Statement of Purpose of the Kennett Abolitionists," which read:

Resolved,
That we recommend to our southern brethren that the most effectual and expeditious way of putting down abolition at the North is to put it up at the South, by breaking the fetters of the captives, and letting the oppressed go free.

Resolved,
That in the potency of the principles, which, as abolitionists, we have embraced, and in the evidences of the advancement of the cause of universal

emancipation which throng upon us, we find abundant encouragement to persevere in our labors, for down-trodden humanity, and much reason to hope that our efforts, under God, will be crowned with entire success.

Resolved,
That any person who aids in restoring the fugitive to his master and in reimposing the chains of slavery upon a fellow being, whether acting as a public officer or otherwise, are guilty of a crime against freedom, humanity, and religion, and should be regarded as the abettor of a huge and cruel disposition.

Resolved,
That those professed ministers of the gospel, who attempt to justify or palliate the system of American slavery from the scriptures of the Old and New Testaments, are doing more to bring the Bible into disrepute and undermine the faith built upon its glorious truths, than all the avowed and open opponents of Christianity within our land, and we are compelled to look upon them, whatever may be their profession, as in reality the enemies of the religion they profess to love.

—Chandler Darlington, sec'y[197]

At that time, the secretary of the society was Chandler Darlington, and the president was John Cox, both of whom were founding members of LPFM fifteen years later.[198] The antislavery sentiment was heating up, as shown by the powerful statement released by the Kennett Square Anti-Slavery Society. This document was so important that it was included in the program for the 150th Anniversary Celebration of the Longwood Progressive Friends Meeting, held on Sunday, May 22, 2005.[199]

In 1838, the message was clear: mere words were not going to be enough to address slavery—action was going to have to be taken. The stage was set for the coming division among Quakers. Quakers were told they should not be an "accessory to this enormous national evil [slavery] but to discourage it by all the justifiable means in their power."[200] Quakers, both liberal and conservative, agreed with this statement. The issue developing was how to put this into practice, especially when it came to being involved with non-Quakers in the antislavery societies.

The divide over whether to become involved with the antislavery movement, was due to some Quakers, thinking similar to the Amish, that they should not be a part of the world and remain to themselves. Other Quakers, however, believed that in order to bring change to the world, you needed to enter the world you were hoping to change. To these Quakers, that meant associating with those worldly, antislavery, non-Quaker people.[201]

The antislavery movement was gaining popularity toward the mid-1800s. In Oxford, Pennsylvania, the Clarkson Anti-Slavery Society was formed in 1832, making it the first such society in Southern Chester County. Most of the members were Quakers. Other societies followed, including Kennett and the Chester County Societies. The division was widening among Quakers, as evidenced by the fact most of the members of these societies were Quakers.[202]

Conservative Quakers were not pleased with progressive Quakers joining "worldly" antislavery societies, but that was not the main issue. Progressive Quakers wanted other Quakers to learn about these societies and how they were helping the cause of abolition and emancipation. To accomplish this, speakers were invited to come present during meetings. Conservatives were against this because, first, the speaker was getting paid, and second, the speaker was reading a speech, thereby speaking by the power of man and not by the leading of the spirit.[203] Bottom line: they were paid to speak, not led to speak.

In response to the issue of paid speakers, Jesse Kersey, a well-known Chester County Quaker wrote:

> I have seen there is a disposition to be doing something by taking an active part with those who are not of us; and who, instead of waiting for the Divine Guide to put them forth, are always ready; and as these run unsent, they cannot prosper the work....There is some reason to believe that many of them [paid lecturers] are acting from no higher or better motive than to have employment of some degree of respectability, and to acquire applause.[204]

To further the divide between conservatives and progressives was the fact that progressive Quakers "judged other friends not by standards of plainness but on how consistently they pleaded the case of the slave, and increasingly saw their opponents for all intents and purposes, pro-slavery."[205] Progressive Quakers believed each Quaker should utilize every chance to vocalize their opposition to slavery. Along with being vocal, progressive Quakers believed action needed to be taken, whether that meant being a part of an antislavery society or assisting freedom seekers in any possible.

"By 1844, the abolitionist-minded friends in Western Quarterly Meeting were growing increasingly impatient with the leadership of the Society of Friends."[206] Increasingly, it was becoming Quakerism versus activism. Progressive Quakers were finding it more and more difficult to merely sit idly by and allow slavery to continue. The annual meeting of the Chester County Anti-Slavery Society was held in August 1844. As usual, the meeting was held at the Marlborough Meeting. This was an antislavery meeting with members who were almost exclusively Quaker—held in a Quaker meetinghouse—to discuss "the pro-slavery character of the Society of Friends and whether it was the duty of reformers to come out of the tainted churches."[207]

As progressive Quakers became more vocal and active in the antislavery movement, conservative Quakers expressed concern over whether "those" Quaker should be allowed to meet in the traditional meetinghouses.[208] So, Conservative Quakers were questioning if the progressive Quakers should be allowed to use traditional meetinghouses for their meetings. And progressive Quakers were questioning if they should continue meeting with the conservatives.

East Fallowfield Riot and People's Hall

Making matters worse was the "East Fallowfield Riot." At a January 1845 meeting, Dr. Edwin Fussell, a progressive antislavery Quaker and the brother of Dr. Bartholomew Fussell, attempted to address the meeting and was met with opposition. Members demanded he be thrown out of the building, and the meeting fell into chaos. After this, the Fallowfield Meeting met to decide if other groups or people (antislavery Quakers and antislavery non-Quaker speakers) should use the meetinghouse, or if it should be kept strictly for Quaker meetings.[209] The Fallowfield Meeting made the decision to ban the East Fallowfield Anti-Slavery Society from holding further meetings.[210]

Upon being banned from holding further society meetings in the Fallowfield Meetinghouse, the society purchased a building lot and erected a building. This was the beginning of the People's Hall. It was first used for the East Fallowfield Anti-Slavery Meetings. Today, various civic groups and organizations use the building.

PEOPLE'S HALL

People's Hall is located ten and a half miles from the author's home. After being banned from the East Fallowfield Meetinghouse, members of the East Fallowfield Anti-Slavery Society built their own place in which to hold society meetings. Isabella Stokes wrote a poem in tribute to this event: "One old building still stands / As a tribute to voices now stilled / It stands as a monument to old 'Friends' / Who dared to do right."[211]

802 Doe Run Road
East Fallowfield Township, PA 19320
484-247-4279
Peopleshall845@gmail.com
Call for an appointment to view the hall.

Another event occurred that increased the desire to form an independent meeting. An unauthorized meeting was held at the Kennett Meeting in August 1851. In November, William Barnard was disowned for "disorderly conduct in having associated with others to hold a meeting out of order and in subversion of the society."[212]

After being banned from the East Fallowfield Meeting, members of the East Fallowfield Anti-Slavery Society built their own meeting place: People's Hall. *Author's collection.*

The more conservative Quakers did not approve of the radical, "worldly," abolitionist, activist Quakers who were vocal about their opposition to slavery and the need for immediate emancipation. Local Quaker meetings took action and disowned a number of their members, including Isaac Mendenhall, John and Hannah Cox, Eusebius and Sarah Barnard, Moses and Mary Pennock, Samuel and Deborah Pennock and others.[213] These disowned Quakers and others decided it might be time to form their own meeting.

MARLBOROUGH RIOT

In 1845, there was the East Fallowfield Riot. Seven years later, there was the Marlborough Riot. It had been announced that Oliver Johnson, the editor of the *Pennsylvania Freeman*, a well-known abolitionist and staunch supporter of the Progressive Quakers, was to address the meeting on First Day—usually a time for worship, not lectures. Already, there were disagreements concerning who should be holding meetings—the conservatives or the progressives— and if First Day Meetings should be exclusively for worship.

The conservatives were prepared to not allow Oliver Johnson to speak. Johnson began to speak and was told by an elder to sit down and stop speaking. Johnson did not sit down and tried to speak again. The constable, who had been asked by the conservatives to be there, was asked to remove Johnson. Eusebius Barnard "and others protested the action, crying 'shame, shame.'"[214] The band of conservatives who did not want Johnson to speak left, and those who remained were able to listen to Johnson speak. Called the Marlborough Riot, this incident increased the growing division between the conservative and progressive Quakers.

~

MARLBOROUGH MEETINGHOUSE

The Marlborough Meetinghouse is located eleven miles from the author's home. It was there that the Marlborough Riot occurred. Oliver Johnson was to speak at the meeting, but the elders had hired a constable in the event that this took place. When Johnson stood to speak, he was told to sit down He was told a second time to sit, refused and, at that time, was arrested.

Marlborough Meetinghouse
843 Marlborough Spring Road
Kennett Square, PA 19348
610-347-8843
Stilwts0023@hotmail.com
This is an active meeting, and you can call ahead to see about attending
"First Day—Sabbath" (Sunday) service.

Finally, an event occurred that all but guaranteed the progressives would
be branching out on their own. The Philadelphia Yearly Meeting was held
in May 1852, and there, two reports were submitted by the conservative
Quakers and the progressive Quakers of the Western Quarterly Meeting.
The yearly meeting acknowledged the conservative report and ignored the
report sent by the progressives.[215]

Marlborough Meetinghouse was the home of the Marlborough Riot. This incident increased
the growing tensions between conservative and progressive Quakers. *Author's collection.*

During the October 1852 Western Quarterly Meeting, the progressives reported that the report submitted to the Philadelphia Yearly Meeting in May was rejected. At this point, it was decided that it was probably time for the progressives to have their own meeting, "and [they] prepared a call for General Religious Conference to be held at the Old Kennett Meeting House on May 22, 1853. The call was addressed to all who were interested in a new religious association free of sectarian strictures and dedicated to the cause of human progress."[216]

Many people attended the convention, and it was decided that the progressives needed to form their own meeting: "The Pennsylvania Yearly Meeting of Progressive Friends." As the name implies, the meeting was located in the state of Pennsylvania, the members would be Quakers (friends) and the members would be in keeping with the statement of purpose that was issued by the Kennett Anti-Slavery Society.[217] The new meeting was open "to all who recognize the equal brotherhood of the human family, without regard to sex, color or condition, and who acknowledge the duty of defining and illustrating their faith in God, not by assent to a creed, but lives of personal purity, and works of beneficence and charity to mankind."[218]

Fifty-eight men and women signed the call for the conference and founded the Longwood Progressive Friends Meeting (LPFM). All of them were staunch abolitionists, and many were active in the Underground Railroad. Because of this antislavery activity, many had been disowned by their home meetings for being "too worldly."[219] Most of the founders lived in and around Kennett Square, and they included Isaac and Dinah Mendenhall, Moses and Mary Pennock, Hannah Darlington, Dr. Bartholomew and Rebecca Fussell, John and Hannah Cox, Eusebius and Sarah Barnard and Amos Preston (Ann Preston's father).[220] This band of fifty-eight believed that "good works are the outward, and faith the inward life of man; they were anxious to live their religion by aiding the fugitive slave."[221]

Many of the founders were involved with various antislavery societies, including the American Anti-Slavery Society (Dr. Fussell was a founding member), the Philadelphia Anti-Slavery Society (Dr. Fussell was a founding member), the Chester County Anti-Slavery Society (Isaac Mendenhall was the treasurer) and the Kennett Anti-Slavery Society (Chandler Darlington was the secretary, and John Cox was the president).

John and Hannah Cox owned the Longwood Farm, which was one of the stations on the Underground Railroad. John and Hannah had been

Old Kennett Meetinghouse disowned a number of its members for their work with the Underground Railroad and holding radical abolitionist views. *Author's collection.*

members of the Old Kennett Friends Meeting but were disowned because of their work with the Underground Railroad, as well as their "radical" abolitionist views.

⌒

OLD KENNETT MEETINGHOUSE

The Old Kennett Meetinghouse is 11.1 miles from the author's home. This meetinghouse is open for worship on the last Sundays of June, July and August. In 1974, it was placed in the National Register of Historic Places.

Old Kennett Meetinghouse
1013 East Baltimore Pike
Kennett Square, PA 19348
old.kennett1710@hotmail.lcom
www.kennettfriends.org

⌒

In 1854, the newly established LPFM was informed that it could no longer meet at the Old Kennett Meeting House. At this point, it approached John and Hannah Cox to see if they would sell some land on which to build a meetinghouse. They agreed, and a parcel of land was purchased from them for $107.11. Once the land was obtained, the construction of the meetinghouse began in earnest, and in nine short months, the building was dedicated on May 19, 1855.[222]

The founding and establishment of LPFM was described in the *Philadelphia Record* on May 6, 1906:

> *Longwood Meeting House, erected about 1854, also figured in the Underground Railroad movement. It was long the center of radicalism as well as culture. It was erected by Quakers who would not keep silent on the subject of slavery. Many of the ardent abolitionists, among them the Coxes and Isaac Mendenhall, were disowned from their own meetings because of their views. These were the new members of the Progressive Meeting of Friends at Longwood.*[223]

The founding members of LPFM believed it was more important to follow a "higher law" when the law of the land contradicted what the "higher law" instructed. Lucretia Mott, a Quaker abolitionist, often shared her well-known motto: "Truth for authority, not authority for truth." The belief she advocated was embraced by many Quakers: a person should not blindly follow the laws of the land just because lawmakers made them, especially if these laws were contrary to your own belief system. Whenever she spoke at the meetinghouse, she would encourage attendees to "search themselves to find what was True, and finding Truth, do their duty to God and humankind."[224]

The Longwood Progressive Friends Meeting enjoyed an eighty-seven-year-long existence. Things were changing in the world, and in 1940, the decision was made to discontinue the meeting. Pierre S. DuPont purchased the

Lucretia Mott was a frequent speaker at LPFM and encouraged her listeners to not blindly follow laws just because lawmakers made them. *Courtesy of the Chester County History Center.*

building, and after sitting vacant for many years, it was transformed into the Brandywine Valley Tourism Information Center.

The abolitionist movement was definitely strengthened by the work of the LPFM. LPFM provided education for both Quakers and non-Quakers alike, as meeting members lectured and met with local groups to discuss slavery and solutions to the issue. Politicians, both on a local and national level, were met with to discuss the importance and need for immediate emancipation. One of those politicians LPFM met with was President Abraham Lincoln, and that meeting and the outcome of it will be discussed later in the chapter.[225]

LPFM AND FAMOUS SPEAKERS

LPFM was home to a variety of speakers who came from far and wide to spread their message, including Frederick Douglass, Harriet Beecher Stowe, John Greenleaf Whittier, Sojourner Truth, Susan B. Anthony and others.[226]

FREDERICK DOUGLASS AND LPFM

The abolitionists and Underground Railroad stationmasters and agents of Southern Chester County were well acquainted with Frederick Douglass. Douglass not only spoke at LPFM, but he also spoke at Hosanna Meeting House and the Oxford Clarkson Anti-Slavery Society meetings. He had escaped slavery and was a passionate orator about the evils of slavery and the need to end it. Abolitionists held up Frederick Douglass as "a living counterexample to slaveholders' arguments that slaves lacked the intellectual capacity to function as independent American citizens."[227] Douglass was frequently criticized for his willingness to meet with anyone to discuss the issues surrounding slavery, abolitionism and emancipation—this even included slaveowners. In response to this criticism, Douglass would counter, "I would unite with anybody to do right and with nobody to do wrong."[228]

Frederick Douglass had escaped slavery and spoke wherever he could about the evils of slavery and the need to end it. *Courtesy of the Chester County History Center.*

HARRIET BEECHER STOWE AND LPFM

Harriet Beecher Stowe was well known for her novel *Uncle Tom's Cabin* and was well received as a speaker at LPFM. Her novel helped those who, until that time, viewed abolitionists as "extremists" understand the plight of the enslaved. Many, especially in the North, felt that because they did not own enslaved people nor knew anybody who did, slavery was not their problem and was therefore not something they needed to be concerned about.

Stowe abhorred slavery. She had watched the politics, read the newspapers, listened to sermons and observed debates on how best to end slavery. She believed what was needed was a way to reach the common man and change public opinion and understanding of the institution of slavery. Stowe felt that if she could touch the souls of man through her writing, she might be able to bring about change. Thus, the beginnings of *Uncle Tom's Cabin* stirred within her. When it was completed, published and released to the public, *Uncle Tom's Cabin* accomplished what Lincoln said was more important than making statutes: "it molded public opinion."[229]

The abolitionists welcomed the novel because it helped bring to light how unjust the Fugitive Slave Act of 1850 was. Frederick Douglass said "the touching, but too truthful tale of *Uncle Tom's Cabin* has kindled the slumbering embers of anti-slavery zeal into active flames. Its recitals have baptized with holy fire myriads who before cared nothing for the bleeding slave."[230]

Stowe was known as an advocate for the Quaker concept of a "higher law"—people sometimes need to follow a "higher law" rather than the laws of the land, especially if the man-made laws are contrary to the "higher law." Of the higher law concept and Stowe, Douglass wrote, "We doubt if abler arguments have ever been presented in favor of the 'Higher Law' that may be found here [in] Mrs. Stowe's truly great work."[231] Booker T. Washington said, "The value of *Uncle Tom's Cabin* to the cause of abolition can never be justly estimated [because] it so stirred the hearts of the northern people that a large part of them were ready either to vote or, in the last extremity, to fight for the suppression of slavery."[232]

Uncle Tom's Cabin helped those who until its publication viewed abolitionists as "extremists" understand the plight of enslaved people. *Courtesy of the Library of Congress.*

HARRIET BEECHER STOWE

Harriet Beecher Stowe and the author are cousins. The Lanyons and the Beechers lived in Litchfield, Connecticut, and were friends. The author's great-grandfather Herbert Beecher Lanyon was named after Harriet Beecher.

So powerful was the effect Stowe's novel had on the nation that when she was visiting President Abraham Lincoln, it is reported he told her, "[So,] you are the woman who wrote the book that started this great war."[233] When the Civil War ended, which resulted in the loss of 623,000 soldiers, Stowe rejoiced, "not that the Union had been preserved, but that slavery had been abolished."[234]

When Stowe was asked what she thought about the effect of the book, she wrote:

> *The effects of the book, so far have been, I think, these: 1ˢᵗ to soften and moderate the bitterness of feeling in extreme abolitionists. 2ⁿᵈ to convert to abolitionists views many whom the same bitterness had repelled. 3ʳᵈ to inspire the free colored people with self-respect, hope, and confidence. 4ᵗʰ to inspire universally through the country a kindlier feeling toward the negro race.*[235]

JOHN GREENLEAF WHITTIER AND LPFM

John Greenleaf Whitter was a Quaker abolitionist, and as such, he was committed to "a cause that he deemed morally correct and socially necessary." Along with Dr. Bartholomew Fussell, Whittier was a founding member of the American Anti-Slavery Society. Whittier personally knew many of the Underground Railroad agents, stationmasters and abolitionists in the Kennett Square area and was always a welcome speaker at LPFM.[236]

When he was speaking at LPFM, he often stayed with John and Hannah Cox at their home. On the occasion of the Coxes' fiftieth wedding

John Greenleaf Whittier was a frequent speaker at LPFM and a founding member of the American Anti-Slavery Society. *Courtesy of the Chester County History Center.*

anniversary, Whittier wrote them a poem to celebrate the times he had with them, the friends he had spent time with at their house and, most importantly, to remember the mission they all partook in. The poem read:

> *How gladly would I tread again the old remembered places,*
> *Sit down beside your hearth once more, and look in the dear old faces;*
> *And thank you for the lessons of your fifty years are teaching,*
> *For honest lives that louder speak than half our noisy preaching;*
> *For works of love and duty that knew no selfish ends,*
> *For hearts and doors set open for the bondman and his friends;*
> *For your steady faith and courage in that dark and evil time*
> *When the Golden Rule was treason, and to feed the hungry, crime;*
> *For the poor slave's house of refuge when the hounds were on his track,*
> *And saint and sinner, church and state, joined hands to send him back.*
> *Blessings upon you! What you did for each sad suffering one,*
> *So homeless and faint and naked, unto our Lord was done!*[237]

SOJOURNER TRUTH AND LPFM

I Sell the Shadow to Support the Substance.
SOJOURNER TRUTH.

Born Isabella Baumfree, Sojourner Truth believed God had called her to travel (or sojourn) and preach the truth about slavery and the need to abolish it. *Courtesy of the Library of Congress.*

Sojourner Truth was born Isabella Baumfree and was born into slavery. In 1826, she escaped from slavery. In 1828, she went to court to try to get her son back from the slave owner. She won the case and became the first Black woman to do so. Isabella "Belle" converted to Methodism. In 1843, she believed God was calling her to travel and preach the truth about slavery and the need for the abolition of slavery. So, she changed her name to Sojourner (traveling) Truth (speaking the truth about slavery and abolitionism). When asked why and what she was doing, she simply replied, "The Spirit calls me, and I must go."[238]

As a formerly enslaved person, Sojourner Truth spoke with great passion about her time being enslaved and was a welcome speaker at LPFM. One time, when she was speaking at LPFM, she said a few opening remarks and then simply sang to get her point across to the people attending:

I pity the slave-mother, careworn and weary,
Who sighs as she presses her babe to her breast;
I lament her sad fate, all so helpless and dreary,
I lament for her woes, and her wrongs unredressed.
O! who can imagine her heart's deep emotion,
As she thinks of her children about to be sold;
You may picture the bound of the rock-girded ocean,
But the grief of that mother can never be told.[239]

SUSAN B. ANTHONY AND LPFM

Susan B. Anthony is best known as a champion for women's rights. However, she was also a staunch abolitionist. Her Quaker parents were also staunch abolitionists. Born a Quaker, by the age of seventeen, she was actively soliciting signatures for antislavery petitions. She was active in the American Anti-Slavery Society, of which Dr. Bartholomew Fussell was a founding member, and was the New York state agent.[240]

Susan B. Anthony and Samuel Pennock's wife, Deborah, were friends. Susan would stay with the Pennocks when she was speaking at LPFM. *Courtesy of the Chester County History Center.*

In 1851, Anthony and Elizabeth Cady Stanton began working together on social reform issues. The Women's Loyal National League was founded by these two women in 1863. Under their direction, this league "conducted the largest petition drive in the United States history up to that time, collecting nearly 400,000 signatures in support of the abolition of slavery." Three years later, the two women, under their organization, the American Equal Rights Association, "campaigned for equal rights for women and African Americans."[241]

Samuel Pennock's wife, Deborah, was an abolitionist, was active with the Underground Railroad and was involved with the women's suffrage movement. Deborah and Susan B. Anthony were friends. Anthony would often stay with the Pennocks when she was speaking at LPFM.[242] Susan B. Anthony was a welcome speaker at LPFM.

LPFM AND PRESIDENT ABRAHAM LINCOLN

LPFM members believed actions truly spoke louder than words. With that in mind, on June 20, 1862, three men and three women from LPFM went to meet with President Lincoln, Eusebius Barnard, Lincoln's cousin; Thomas Garrett; and Dinah Mendenhall. The group was well received by President Lincoln, partially because he came from a Quaker background and partially because LPFM members, unlike other Quakers, realized the Constitution of the United States mandated President Lincoln to keep the United States intact, even if that meant going to war.

Eusebius Barnard told President Lincoln that the delegation truly hoped he would, "under diving guidance, be led to free the slaves," to which Lincoln responded he would, "with a firm reliance upon the Divine arm and seeking light from above, to do his duty in the place to which he had been called."[243] The memorial (petition) that the members of LPFM presented to President Lincoln reads as follows:

Memorial to the President

To Abraham Lincoln, President of the United States,
The Religious Society of Friends, in yearly meeting assembled at Longwood, Chester County, from the 5th to the 7th of the sixth month, 1862, under a solemn sense of the perils besetting the country, and the duty of devolving upon them to exert whatever influence they possess to rescue it from the impending destruction, beg leave respectfully but earnestly, to set forth the consideration of President Lincoln—

That they fully share in the general grief and reprobation felt at the seditious course pursued in opposition to the general government by the so-called "Confederate States" regarding it as marked by all the revolting features of high-handed robbery, cruel treachery, and murderous violence, and therefore utterly to be abhorred and condemned by every lover of his country and every friend of the human race.

That, nevertheless, this sanguinary rebellion finds its cause, purpose, and combustible materials in that most unchristian and barbarous system of slavery which prevails in that section of the country and in the guilt of which the whole land has long been deeply involved by general complicity, so that it is to be contritely recognized as the penalty due to such persistent, flagrant transgression, and as the inevitable operation of the law of eternal justice.

That thus heavily visited for its grinding oppression of an unfortunate face, "peeled, meted out, and trodden under foot" whose wrongs have so long cried unto heaven for redress, and thus solemnly warned of the infatuation as well as exceeding wickedness of endeavoring to secure peace, prosperity, and unity, while leaving millions to clank their chains in the house of bondage, the nations, in its official organization should lose no time in proclaiming immediate and universal emancipation, so that the present frightful effusion of blood may cease, liberty be established, and permanent reconciliation effected by the removal of the sole cause of these divisions.

That in his speech delivered in Springfield, before his election to the office of chief magistrate, the president expressly declared, "A house divided against itself cannot stand. I believe this government cannot endure permanently have slave and half free. I do not expect the Union to be dissolved—I do not expect the house to fall—but I do expect it will cease to be divided. It will become all one thing, or all the other."

That this society, therefore, urgently unites with a widespread and constant increasing sentiment in beseeching the presidents, as the head of the nation, clothed with the constitutional power in such a fearful emergency, to suppress the rebellion effectually by the removal of its cause, not to allow the present golden opportunity to pass without decreeing the entire abolition of slavery throughout the land, as a measure imperatively demanded by a due regard for the unity of the country, the safety and happiness of the people, the preservation of free institutions, and by every consideration of justice, mercy, and peace. Otherwise, we have fearful reason to apprehend that blood will continue to flow and fierce dissensions to abound, and calamities increase, and fiery judgements to be poured out, until the work of national destruction is consummated beyond hope of recovery.

Within a few months, Lincoln issued the Emancipation Proclamation, which took effect on January 1, 1863.[244]

Longwood Progressive Friends truly affected the abolitionist movement. The members of LPFM were ardent abolitionists, and many were active in the Underground Railroad. "While the majority of friends believed that slavery was wrong because it enslaved God's children, the progressives went further by actively lobbying for emancipation....The Progressive Friends paved the way for the Emancipation Proclamation and the 13th, 14th, and 15th Amendments to the United States Constitution."[245]

THE CIVIL WAR AMENDMENTS

General Robert E. Lee surrendered to General Ulysses S. Grant on April 9, 1865. On April 11, 1865, President Abraham Lincoln gave his "Speech on Reconstruction," which was the president's last public speech. He spoke about bringing the North and the South back together and working together to help the nation recover from the destruction and devastation of the Civil War. This was going to be a challenging time for President Lincoln and the nation. One of the largest challenges was how to help 4 million formerly enslaved people assimilate into society. The other formidable task was the question of how the southern states were going to be reconnected to the Union.[246]

In the crowd, listening to the president was John Wilkes Booth, a southern sympathizer who was furious as he listened to the speech. He vowed he would kill the president. True to his word, on April 14, Booth shot the president while Lincoln was sitting in Ford's Theater. The next day, the president died from his wounds.[247]

The Thirteenth, Fourteenth and Fifteenth Amendments are referred to as the Civil War amendments because they all became law shortly after the Civil War ended. These amendments ended slavery, granted citizenship to those born in the United States or who are naturalized and granted the right to vote to every male citizen. Women would not have the right to vote until 1920 with the ratification of the Nineteenth Amendment. "Congress required former Confederate states to ratify [all three of the Civil War Amendments] as a condition of regaining federal representation."[248]

Thirteenth Amendment

The Thirteenth Amendment was ratified on December 6, 1865. The question of slavery had yet to be resolved prior to 1865. With the passage of the Thirteenth Amendment, slavery was abolished nationally. The amendment comprised two sections:

> *Section 1. Neither slavery nor involuntary servitude, except as punishment for crime whereof the party shall have been duly convicted, shall exist within the United States, or any place subject to their jurisdiction.*

> *Section 2. Congress shall have power to enforce this article by appropriate legislation.*[249]

Fourteenth Amendment

The Fourteenth Amendment granted citizenship to all persons. This amendment was ratified on July 9, 1868. The Fourteenth Amendment comprised five sections. Section 2 said that both Black and White people were to be counted as whole persons. Section 3 "excluded many former Confederate officers or officials from holding office."[250] Section 4 verified Congress's intent to repay Civil War public debts. Section 5 had an enforcement clause like the Thirteenth Amendment.

Section 1 stated:

> *All persons, born or naturalized in the United States, and subject to the jurisdiction thereof, are citizens of the United States and the state wherein they reside;*
>
> *No state shall make or enforce any law which shall abridge the privileges or immunities of citizens of the United States;*
>
> [No state] *shall deprive any person of life, liberty, or property, without due process of law, [and that];*
>
> [No state] *shall deny to any person within its jurisdiction the equal protection of the laws.*[251]

Fifteenth Amendment

On March 30, 1869, the Fifteenth Amendment to the United State Constitution was ratified and read:

> *Section 1. The right of citizens of the United States to vote shall not be denied or abridged by the Unites States or by any state on account of race, color, or previous condition of servitude.*
>
> *Section 2. The Congress shall have the power to enforce this article with appropriate legislation.*[252]

Women would not gain the right to vote until August 1920, when the Nineteenth Amendment was ratified. Susan B. Anthony and Frederick Douglass were good friends and worked together in the fight for the rights of the enslaved and women. Anthony wanted the right for women to vote to be put into the Fifteenth Amendment. Douglass argued that Congress would never pass both, and he felt that the right for free Black men to vote was more important at the time. Anthony reluctantly agreed.

LONGWOOD PROGRESSIVE FRIENDS MEETINGHOUSE TODAY

The LPFM Meetinghouse and the cemetery, which is just across the street from the meetinghouse, are both owned by Longwood Gardens. The Brandywine Valley Tourism Information Center is housed in the meetinghouse. There are very knowledgeable volunteers there who can inform visitors about Kennett Square, the Underground Railroad, the Quakers and the abolitionist movement.

Today, the Longwood Progressive Friends Meetinghouse is home to the Brandywine Valley Tourism Information Center. *Author's collection.*

Local Graves

Top: The grave and headstone of Isaac and Dinah Mendenhall—two of the best-known abolitionists and Underground Railroad members. *Author's collection.*

Bottom: The Harriet Tubman Underground Railroad Byway starts in Maryland. One of its destinations is the LPFM. *Author's collection.*

The Longwood Progressive Friends Meetinghouse has a cemetery that can be found directly across the street. In this cemetery are the graves of Isaac and Dinah Mendenhall, John and Hannah Cox, Chandler and Hannah Darlington, Dr. Bartholomew Fussell and Eusebius Barnard. It is fitting that they were buried close together, as they worked closely together as members of the Longwood Progressive Friends Meeting, abolitionists and stationmasters of the Underground Railroad.

Both the cemetery and the meetinghouse are listed in the National Register of Historic Places.[253] The meetinghouse and cemetery have also been designated as part of the prestigious National Park Service Network to Freedom. "The National Park Service award comes after a multi-year process of in-depth research and documentation demonstrating that the meetinghouse and cemetery were crucial parts of the Underground Railroad and the campaign to end slavery. The award emphasizes the meetinghouse's local and national importance in Kennett Square's many abolitionist activities from about 1830–1860."[254]

As the National Park Service award stated, the meetinghouse and its members were "crucial parts of the Underground Railroad and the campaign to end slavery." Its members were active in the Underground Railroad, were ardent abolitionists and were willing to meet with President Lincoln to make the case for emancipation. The meetinghouse was a station on the Underground Railroad, and it hosted many national antislavery speakers who helped educate the citizens about the evils of slavery and the need to see it abolished. Furthermore, the Longwood Progressive Friends Meetinghouse is also a stop on the Harriet Tubman Underground Railroad Byway.

᳄ ᳄ ᳄

Up from a small piece of the Cox family farmland rose a building whose members would have a tremendous impact both locally and nationally that would ultimately result in the emancipation of the enslaved and the abolishment of slavery.

Not only did Frederick Douglass and Sojourner Truth speak at the Longwood Progressive Friends Meetinghouse, but they also spoke at the Hosanna Church—a little church located in the free Black community of Hinsonville.

5

HINSONVILLE

HISTORY OF HINSONVILLE

In 1830, Emory Hinson, a free Black man from Maryland, purchased eighteen acres of land. This was the beginning of a town named after Hinson: Hinsonville.[255] Hinson purchased his land from a White Quaker named John Leeke. Leeke had sold land to Edward Walls a year earlier, but Walls did not move to Hinsonville at that time. Walls was instrumental in getting his two brothers, William and George, to move to Hinsonville and purchase land there as well.[256]

Along with the three Walls brothers, the three Amos brothers, Samuel H., James Ralston and Thomas Henry, were early settlers there as well.

The town's location was ideal, as it was situated in southern Chester County, a thriving area. The road that the residents of Hinsonville used was the Oxford-Jennersville Road. As commerce grew, so did the population of the region, and the little country road became the main travel route between Baltimore and Philadelphia. This route soon became one of the Underground Railroad routes, and Hinsonville and its residents became active agents for the Underground Railroad.[257]

Hinsonville had a number of Underground Railroad agents, including James Ralston Amos, Thomas Amos, Samuel Glasgow, Emory Hinson, Albert Walls, George Walls and William Walls.[258]

SITE OF HINSONVILLE

The site of Hinsonville is located 5.8 miles from the author's home. Since it was located six miles from the Mason-Dixon line, freedom seekers would often come to Hinsonville for rest, food and a chance to assimilate into the tight-knit community or board the Underground Railroad for their journey to freedom.

James Ralston Amos and his brother Thomas Henry of Hinsonville went on to help cofound with Reverend John Miller Dickey the Ashmun Institute, later renamed Lincoln University.

Thomas Fitzgerald's house and barn were located in Hinsonville and served as a station on the Underground Railroad. Fugitives traveling from Maryland and Virginia would travel the Oxford-Jennersville Road as they journeyed from the Mason-Dixon line. Upon arriving at Thomas's house, the freedom seekers were told they would be able to find shelter in the barn. If the fugitives told Thomas they smoked, they were requested to leave their pipe and tobacco with Thomas. He would tell his visitors they were welcome to share breakfast with him in the morning. However, if they chose to leave prior to dawn, they would find their pipe and tobacco outside the barn. Thomas's only request was that the freedom seekers not burn his barn down.[259]

Although many of the early residents of Hinsonville came from other counties in Pennsylvania, including Chester County, others crossed the Mason-Dixon line. "Hinsonville attracted both free and determined-to-be free people who championed religious independence, higher education, landownership, and equal rights."[260] The town of Hinsonville came into existence thirty-one years before the Civil War began.

Hinsonville was built on the land that was purchased by Edward Walls in 1829, a free Black man from Maryland. The town quickly grew, and by 1845, the residents had built their own church, Hosanna AUMP Church. Much of the growth of the town was due to the emigration of free Black people from Maryland and other southern states.

Many who came to reside in Hinsonville came from the state of Maryland, as the 1850 census showed. A large number of residents over the age of forty listed their place of birth as Maryland. This made sense because more and more restructure legislation was being passed by the state of Maryland. For example, free black people were required to carry proof of their status or risk being arrested and enslaved.[261] Another law stated that Black individuals who left the state for longer than thirty days without informing government officials were not allowed back into the state of Maryland.[262]

The town's original families came from three states: Maryland, Delaware and Pennsylvania. The Maryland families included the Wallses, Jays, Coles, Hinsons and Davises. The Delaware families included Elias Draper, the Fitzgeralds and Rachel Walls, George's wife. The Pennslvania families included the Amoses, the Glasgows and the Hiltons.[263] Of those families, four of them were the center of the community of Hinsonville: the Amoses, Glasgows, Wallses and Hinsons.[264]

Family life was the number-one priority in the Black community. So, it made sense that Hinsonville became a place to immigrate to. Here was a place where family roots could be planted and families torn apart by slavery could be reunited. The wonderful phenomenon was the definition of *family*. Family not only included blood relatives, but it also included those who had no blood-related family. Those who carried the wounds of slavery were helped with their healing by being incorporated into the family unit.

Hinsonville was transforming into an independent society and an independent family life structure. No longer were slave owners dictating how life should be lived and what family was to look like. Residents were free to pursue their dreams without having to have those dreams dictated by owners or employers. Whether they were fleeing from the slave state of Maryland or they were free from Chester County, the desire to live in a safe community with other Black people must have been a tremendous motivating factor to make Hinsonville home.

Many settling in Hinsonville had been denied the right to the fruits of their labor. No longer would another person take what was theirs and what they had produced. The freedom Hinsonville offered meant others could no longer "discipline, sell, and transport them [Hinsonville residents] against their will."[265] Town residents could decide if and when to marry, if and when to have children, if and when to educate their children and where and how to work. This meant free, freed and freedom-seeking Black people could live together in a community that offered many of the freedoms previously denied.[266]

Hinsonville lasted for about forty years. During that time, it provided the opportunity for free, freed and freedom-seeking Black to escape "slave-state oppression and free-state prejudice."[267] The town provided Black people the opportunity to live together, support one another and learn skills they could take into the greater community.

In the end, Hinsonville provided an example of what family life looked like, what it meant to care for all members of the community, what it meant to welcome freedom seekers into the arms of fellowship and what it meant to desire a church and build one. During a time of great turmoil in the country, Hinsonville was able to provide its members with a sense of stability.

HINSONVILLE AND LINCOLN UNIVERSITY

When the Ashmun Institute (later renamed Lincoln University, after President Lincoln's assassination) began construction, the residents of Hinsonville were excited and assisted in different ways. The women fed the workers. The men helped with the construction. In the beginning, nobody could have known what would happen. The pursuit of a higher education seemed like such a wonderful goal, but it turned into the very thing that ultimately ended Hinsonville. Hinsonville was not like other towns that were abandoned and fell into ruin. Instead, the oldest historically Black degree-granting university in the United States ended up taking over the very village of Hinsonville.[268]

Hinsonville began as a farming community and maintained that lifestyle for forty years until the university overtook the farms as it continued to expand. Between the ever-growing university and the new railroad line, Hinsonville vanished.

The ever-expanding university "bought up the land of the early residents." Needing land on which to build the Ashmun Institute, Reverend John Miller Dickey purchased thirty acres from a White farmer named John Powell. The land was part of the farm that originally belonged to Emory Hinson.[269]

More and more Hinsonville residents sold their property to the university. As the university began to grow, Hinsonville began to shrink. George Glasgow had a little store across the way from Hosanna Meeting House. Glasgow died in 1868, and the university quickly purchased the property and tore the store down. Draper's Store was the other local Hinsonville store. In 1871, the university bought the store and land. Today, the Mary Dod Brown Memorial Chapel sits on the site of that store. So much expansion took place that "when the second post–Civil War atlas of Chester County was published by Witmer in 1873, not only had the name Hinsonville disappeared, the very crossroads to which the name had been attached had ceased to exist."[270]

In the end, you had a Black university taking over a Black community. From the ashes of a town no longer in existence rose a university that would have a profound effect on the world. The university's first graduates would go to Africa as missionaries. Once the Civil War ended, the university played a new role of providing education for freed people.

HINSONVILLE MEN AND THE UNION ARMY

The Emancipation Proclamation provided the opportunity for Black people to enlist in the Union army. It was on January 1, 1863, that the Emancipation Proclamation stated, "Such persons [that is, African American men] of suitable condition, will be received into the armed serves of the United States."[271] Realizing this, there was a concerted effort to enlist them. This was an important time in the life of Black men because, as Frederick Douglass declared once, "the Black man gets upon his person the brass letters, U.S.… he has earned the right to citizenship in the United States."[272]

In southern Chester County, the Quakers were mixed on their opinion of war. Quakers believed in ending slavery, but some were not in favor of war due to the Quaker tradition of being antimilitary. While Quakers as a whole believed in emancipation, some Quakers took action. This was the case with the members of the Longwood Progressive Friends. Some of the members met with President Lincoln to request he support emancipation.[273]

Black residents in southern Chester County supported the Civil War. Until the Emancipation Proclamation became law, Black Americans could only serve as laborers. As soon as they could, many enlisted as soldiers in the Union army. Eighteen Hinsonville men enlisted in the Union army:[274]

Samuel Henry Blake, 127th Pennsylvania
Charles William Cole, 24th Pennsylvania
James Cole, 54th Massachusetts
Josiah Cole, 54th Massachusetts
Amos Daws, 127th Pennsylvania
George W. Duffy, 22nd Pennsylvania
Robert G. Fitzgerald, 54th Massachusetts
William B. Fitzgerald, 41st Pennsylvania
Hugh Hall, 25th Pennsylvania
Isaac Amos Hollingsworth, 127th Pennsylvania
Wesley Jay, 54th Massachusetts

Lewis Palmer, 25th Pennsylvania
Stephen J. Ringgold, 22nd Pennsylvania
Lewis W. Ringgold, 25th Pennsylvania
Abraham Stout, 41st Pennsylvania
Albert G. Walls, 54th Massachusetts

FIFTY-FOURTH MASSACHUSETTS VOLUNTEER INFANTRY REGIMENT

Six of the eighteen Hinsonville men enlisted in the Fifty-Fourth Massachusetts Volunteer Infantry Regiment. Josiah and James Cole were first cousins of Albert G. Walls. George, Wesley and William Jay were brothers. Of the six enlistees, five returned after their service to Hinsonville. On July 16, 1863, during the Battle of Sol Legare Island, near Charleston, South Carolina, Albert Walls went missing and has always been presumed to have been killed during this battle. He was buried in the cemetery at Hosanna Church, and a special memorial has been placed there. Shortly after President Lincoln issued the Emancipation Proclamation, the governor of Massachusetts John A. Andrew, a staunch abolitionist, was the first official to put forth a call for Black soldiers to enlist in the Union army. The response was overwhelming, seeing as Massachusetts's Black population was extremely small. Two weeks after the call went out, over one thousand Black men were enlisted. Included in that one thousand men were two sons of Frederick Douglass: Charles and Lewis Douglass.[275]

Black men comprised the Fifty-Fourth Massachusetts Volunteer Infantry Regiment, making it the first such regiment in the North to participate in the Civil War. Based on the record of the Fifty-Fourth Massachusetts, Union army recruiters were more willing to seek out Black men to join the Union army. This resulted in the Union army and navy being made up of ten percent Black soldiers.

The Fifty-Fourth Massachusetts Volunteer Infantry Regiment was comprised of 1,007 Black soldiers and 37 White officers. The Fifty-Fourth gathered on the morning of May 28, 1863, on the Boston Common to be sent off to battle in the South. This was truly an act of courage, as the Confederate congress has announced "every captured Black solider would be sold into slavery, and every white officer in command of Black troops would be executed."[276]

Governor Andrew told the troops, "I know not where in all human history to any given thousand men in arms there has been committed a work at once so proud, so precious, so full of hope and glory as the work committed to you."[277] Later that day the Fifty-Fourth headed to Charleston, South Carolina.

On July 18, 1863, Colonel Shaw led 600 of his men into the Battle for Fort Wagner. Prior to going into battle, Colonel Shaw told his soldiers, "I want you to prove yourselves. The eyes of thousands will look on what you do tonight."[278] Shaw was instantly killed, and 280 of the 600 soldiers were killed. The Confederates threw all 280 Black soldiers and 1 White officer into a single unmarked grave. They then sent a telegram to the Union military, stating, "We have buried [Shaw] with his n——s."[279] While they thought this would discourage White officers from joining Black soldiers

Albert Walls went missing during the Battle of Sol Legare near Charleston, South Carolina, and it's always been presumed he was killed in battle. *Author's collection.*

in battle, it actually backfired, and White officers continued working with Black soldiers. The parents of Colonel Shaw told the press they could think of "no holier place" for their son to be buried than "surrounded by…brave and devoted soldiers."[280]

For the next two years, the Fifty-Fourth Massachusetts Volunteer Infantry Regiment was involved in battles in South Carolina, Georgia and Florida. Finally, the Fifty-Fourth made its triumphal return to Boston in September 1865.

The work of the Fifty-Fourth resulted in two consequences. First, prior to Black men joining the Union army, leadership was unsure of the abilities of Black soldiers. The heroic actions of the Fifty-Fourth during the Battle of Fort Wagner quickly squelched that uncertainty. Second, because of the result of the Battle of Fort Wagner, the number of Black men enlisting in the Union army dramatically increased, almost reaching a total of two hundred thousand by 1865.[281]

The Fifty-Fourth Massachusetts Volunteer Infantry Regiment, including the six heroic men of Hinsonville, were able to prove, once and for all, that Black men were equal to the White soldiers of the Union army.

✷ ✷ ✷

Hinsonville provided a place for families to grow up together, no longer having to fear what would happen in the environment of a slave state. Free, freed and freedom-seeking black people could live in harmony. When duty called, the men of Hinsonville answered it and served with honor.

Being a part of Hinsonville afforded James Ralston Amos the opportunity to be a part of Hosanna Church and later to meet the Reverend John Miller Dickey. Reverend Dickey and the Hinsonville Community, led by James Ralston Amos and his brother Thomas, would go on to found the Ashmun Institute, later to be renamed Lincoln University.

6

HOSANNA CHURCH

History of Hosanna Meeting House

The Bible speaks of faith, hope and love. Hosanna Church, built in 1843, has been representative of those three spiritual attributes. Hosanna was built in the town of Hinsonville, a community founded by free Black people that is located six miles from the Mason-Dixon line. Hinsonville and Hosanna go hand and hand, as the original settlers of Hinsonville were also the founders of Hosanna.[282]

As the town of Hinsonville grew, so did the needs of the community. Hinsonville was a close community, where everyone knew each other. Family life was the number-one priority, followed by church life. Originally, residents of Hinsonville took turns meeting in each other's homes for Sunday worship, but in 1843, it was decided that it was time to build a church. A building committee was formed that consisted of brothers James, Samuel and Thomas Amos; brothers Edward, George and William Walls; and Samuel Glasgow.[283]

Edward Walls, a free Black man, was one of the largest landowners in Hinsonville. So, the building committee approached Edward, who owned land where they would like to build the church. Edward donated a half-acre on which to build the church.[284]

~

Hosanna Meeting House

The Hosanna Meeting House is located five and a half miles from the author's home.

Hosanna became the focal point of the community of Hinsonville. It provided opportunities for free Black people and freedom seekers living in the community to learn leadership skills. Members of the community rallied together to raise funds to build the little church.

It served as a platform for abolitionists and antislavery leaders to express their views. It also played a role in the Underground Railroad, providing church members the opportunity to assist freedom seekers along their journeys to freedom.

Hosanna Church
531 University Road
Lincoln University, PA 19352
The church is not open at this time.

~

The building committee took it upon itself to fundraise by going out into the neighborhood, soliciting funds, primarily from local White residents. Samuel Glasgow, a brickmaker by trade, most likely provided the bricks with which to build the church. With funding secured and building materials ready, the people of Hinsonville began the task of erecting the church, which they completed and dedicated in 1845.[285]

Slave owners granted time off for their enslaved people. This was usually from noon on Saturday until Sunday evening. Because Hinsonville, where Hosanna was going to be built, was only six miles away from the Mason-Dixon line, the enslaved would come assist in the construction of the church. Once completed, the enslaved and free Black people would gather to worship. Some slave owners did not like their enslaved people attending worship with free Black people because they thought their enslaved came away with an attitude of "uppishness."[286] There was another major reason that slave owners did not want their enslaved attending Sunday service at Hosanna. This is discussed later in the chapter.

Hosanna often held two services on Sunday. The first service was more formal, because the agent of the slave owner was there to keep an eye on his charges. After the agent left, there would be a second service, which was freer and consisted of upbeat music that allowed the congregation to better express themselves to God.[287]

This was an exciting time for the residents of Hinsonville. Some of the residents were free Black people, and others were freedom seekers who had settled down in the community. Some had been victims of the slave trade, some had escaped slavery and many had no history because they did not know their date of birth or place of birth. What so many of the families of Hinsonville wanted was a place that would help them establish their roots.[288] For many residents, family was first, and church was second in importance. This is why the thought of having a church they could call their own was so appealing. To further this feeling of belonging, the church wanted to belong to a denomination.[289] Early on, Hosanna changed its denominational affiliation two or three times, but it finally joined the African Union First Colored Methodist Protestant (AUMP) denomination. Hosanna has continued with AUMP since that time.[290] Although Hosanna has a very small membership today, its number of members from the founding of Ashmun Institute in 1853 until around 1880 proved to be the largest.[291]

Hosanna graveyard was one of the first graveyards where Black people could have the graves of their loved ones marked. *Author's collection.*

After meeting in each other's homes for Sunday service, the residents of Hinsonville decided to build their own church: Hosanna Meeting House. *Author's collection.*

Because there was no town or borough hall for residents to gather in for public meetings, Hosanna Church became the place where all the business of the community of Hinsonville was conducted.

Along with the church building, a graveyard was built. Hosanna graveyard was "one of the first marked grave sites for Blacks" in Southern Chester County.[292] Some of the tombstones of Hosanna members have their African names engraved in the headstone. Among the graves are those of members of the famed Fifty-Fourth Massachusetts Volunteer Infantry Regiment, which gained notoriety at the battle for Fort Wagner in Morris Island, South Carolina. The Fifty-Fourth Massachusetts Regiment fought the Confederates and also fought for equal pay.[293]

With the establishment of the church and the graveyard, and with other needs of the church, various committees were developed. In a time when Black people were not allowed to serve on juries or vote, this became an opportunity for residents of Hinsonville to learn responsibility and develop leadership skills.[294]

Many of the residents of Hinsonville did not own property. Being a part of the church allowed them to feel a sense of ownership. The men were able to help with the construction of the building, and the women formed a ladies' auxiliary. The reputation of the women of Hosanna was becoming well known in the community, as the women went into the community to serve the less fortunate by providing food and clothing, and they cared for those who could not care for themselves.

For both groups, this was a precursor to the building of the Ashmun Institute. The men were able to assist with the construction of institute's buildings, and the women were able to help provide meals. It is believed that the completion of Hosanna served as an impetus to begin the construction of Ashmun. The construction of Hosanna brought the community together in a cohesive fashion, so when the call went out for assistance with the construction of Ashmun, it was a foregone conclusion that this would happen.

The Amos brothers held various roles when it came to Hosanna. Initially, the three brothers helped with fundraising. James was the pastor of Hosanna in the beginning. Samuel, Thomas and James were trustees of Hosanna. Eventually answering God's call, both James and Thomas became ministers. James and Thomas were Underground Railroad agents and were among the first students to enroll and graduate from Ashmun Institute (now known as Lincoln University).

HOSANNA CHURCH AND THE AFRICAN UNION METHODIST PROTESTANT CHURCH (AUMP)

As the membership of the church grew, the need for the church to have its own building was clear. Not only did the members want to have their own church building, but they also wanted to be a part of a denomination to give themselves a sense of belonging and credibility. "Methodism was particularly appealing to Blacks not only because of its religious message about salvation but also because of its early condemnation of slavery."[295]

John Wesley, the founder of Methodism, made his stand on slavery clear when he wrote in 1743:

> *Give liberty to whom liberty is due, that is, to every child of man, to every partaker of human nature. Let none serve you but by his own act and deed, by his own voluntary action. Away with all whips, all chains, all compulsion. Be gentle toward all men; and see that you invariably do with every one as you would he should do unto you.*[296]

Furthermore, John Wesley wrote in his book, *Thoughts on Slavery*: "Freedom is unquestionably the birth right of all mankind; Africans as well as well as Europeans: to keep the former in a state of slavery, is a constant violation of that right, and therefore also of justice."[297]

It is most likely that residents of Hinsonville attended the "Big August Quarterly" in Wilmington, Delaware. In doing so, they learned about the history of Peter Spencer and the exodus from church, with White oversight, to a completely independent and free denomination. The Big August Quarterly was an annual event that was started in 1814 by Peter Spencer. The Big August Quarterly was an opportunity for free Black people and the enslaved to come together for fun, food and fellowship. The Big August Quarterly provided an opportunity for families whose lives had been uprooted by slavery to come together and enjoy each other's company. In the early festival days, Thomas Garrett and Harriet Tubman would be at the festival, willing to place freedom seekers on the Underground Railroad if they were asked to do so.[298] Attendees came from the tri-state area of Maryland, Pennsylvania and Delaware. This festival continues to today, making it "the oldest such celebration in the country."[299]

Prior to the founding of the Union Church of Africans in 1813, Peter Spencer and a group of approximately forty people, in 1805, tired of being under White leadership, left the Asbury Methodist Episcopal Church, a predominately White church. After they broke away and started Ezion Methodist Episcopal Church, they were still under the auspices of the predominately White Methodist Episcopal denomination. Spencer and his congregation were not allowed to choose their own preachers.[300] Wanting autonomy and independence, in 1813, Spencer founded the Union Church of Africans, a denomination that eventually became known as the African Union First Colored Methodist Protestant Church and Connection (AUMP) Church. The Union Church of Africans was "the first African American church independently incorporated in 1813."[301]

The Big August Quarterly is an annual observance of the day Peter Spencer led his people out of White oversight and into an independent denomination. That is why Spencer was known as the "father of the independent Black church movement."[302]

Spencer was an enslaved man from Maryland who obtained his freedom when his master died, and the master's will decreed Spencer was free. Initially, Black people worshipped in White churches and then worshipped on their own—but under the oversight of White people. Black people wanted to have their own churches, overseen by their own ministers and ruling boards. First known as the "African Meeting House," Hosanna formally organized in 1843 as an AUMP church.

Hosanna Church and the Underground Railroad

Not only did Hosanna Church host abolitionist speakers, such as Frederick Douglass and Sojourner Truth, but it also served as a stop on the Underground Railroad. One time when Frederick Douglass was speaking, he "praised the little parish for her work in the field of freedom and self-help."[303] When Harriett Tubman was leading freedom seekers on the Maryland–Oxford route on the Underground Railroad, she utilized Hosanna as one of her stops to receive food, shelter, rest and clothing.

The enslaved were given Saturday afternoon and Sunday off to rest. Many enslaved people came to Hosanna on Sunday mornings for worship service. They were also a part of services and partook in fellowship following the services. If the slave owner was not present, freedom seekers would get on a free Black person's wagon and drive away to be taken to a station on the Underground Railroad—often, the wagon would go to Ann Preston's house in West Grove, Pennsylvania. Sometimes, if slave owners or their guards were on the grounds of the church, church members would provide clothing to make freedom seekers look more like their free counterparts. They would then leave church in the company of other free Black people and drive off under the watchful eye of the guards.

This also occurred on Saturday evenings, when Hosanna hosted antislavery meetings. If a freedom seeker showed up on a Saturday evening while an antislavery meeting was taking place, they would be given a change of clothes to blend in with the attendees. After the meeting, one of the attendees would volunteer to have the freedom seeker ride in their wagon to be transported to a nearby station on the Underground Railroad. If a freedom seeker was being pursued by slave catchers and there was no Saturday or Sunday meeting taking place, they often would hide under the crawl space under the church until it was safe to come out and continue their journey.

The residents of Hinsonville, most of whom were members of Hosanna, reflected the opinion of many of the Quakers living in southern Chester County—they were to assist freedom seekers in their quest for freedom. Aside from using the church, Hinsonville residents allowed freedom seekers to hide in their barns and other outbuildings to escape the watchful eye of slave catchers. Because the residents of Hinsonville were comprised of free Black people and escaped fugitives, there was a willingness to assist others obtain their much-sought-after and desired freedom. The passage of the Fugitive Slave Act of 1850 only helped to solidify their resolve to make sure all was done to ensure freedom for those who were seeking it.

In 2013, Hosanna Church was undergoing renovations. One of the projects was the installation of an indoor bathroom. Prior to that time, there was only an outhouse. As excavation was taking place for the plumbing, a tunnel was discovered. There, freedom seekers could quickly hide from slave catchers and, if need be, crawl through the tunnel, away from the back of the church, and surface in the woods, where their journey could continue.[304]

HOSANNA CHURCH TODAY

The church building is the same as it was when built in 1843. Everything is original, including the pulpit and pastor's chair. The furnace has been replaced, and a new ceiling fan has been installed. As mentioned previously, an indoor bathroom has replaced the outhouse.[305] Hosanna Church and the graveyard are in need of restoration. Hopefully, this historic building and its grounds will be brought back to their former glory and take their place as a significant part of the history of southern Chester County.

THE PENNSYLVANIA HISTORIC MARKER FOR THE HOSANNA CHURCH

On Saturday, May 9, 1992, at 2:30 p.m., there was an event held for the "Dedication of an Official State Historical Marker Honoring Hosanna African Union Methodist Protestant Church." The event was sponsored by the "Pennsylvania Historical and Museum Commission, in cooperation with its Black History Advisory Committee and Lincoln University." The invocation was given by Reverend Andrew Jenkins Jr. "He's Got the Whole

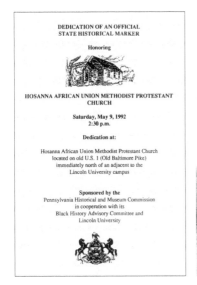

Left: The Dedication Program was held at Hosanna Church. *Author's collection.*

Right: This marker highlights an important historic structure that played a significant role in the lives of those seeking freedom. *Courtesy of the Pennsylvania Historic and Museum.*

World in His Hands" was sung by Genevia Barnett prior to the unveiling of the marker, and then Barnett led the attendees in singing "We Shall Overcome" to close out the event.[306]

BENCH BY THE ROAD PROJECT AND HOSANNA CHURCH

The Bench by the Road Project is a program that was developed by the Toni Morrison Society. In a 1989 interview with *World Magazine*, Toni Morrison, a Black author, expressed her frustration and sadness over the lack of memorials honoring enslaved people.

In this interview, she said:

> There is no place you or I can go, to think about or not think about, to summon the presence of, or recollect the absences of slaves....There is no suitable memorial, or plaque, or wreath, or wall, or park, or skyscraper lobby. There's no 300-foot tower, there's no small bench by the road. There is not even a tree scored, an initial that I can visit or you can visit in Charleston or Savannah or New York or Providence or better still on the banks of the Mississippi.[307]

137

To address this need, the Toni Morrison Society founded the Bench by the Road Project in 1993. The project places "benches and plaques at sites commemorating significant moments, individuals, and locations within the history of the African Diaspora."[308]

The first bench was placed at the African Slave Trade Point of Entry on Sullivan's Island, South Carolina, on July 26, 2008. The twenty-fifth anniversary bench was placed at Howard University in Washington, D.C., on April 5, 2019.

Hosanna Church was the site of the sixteenth bench placement, and that occurred on September 18, 2015. The Friends of Hosanna at Lincoln University submitted the application to the Toni Morrison Society, and it was accepted. Dr. Craig Stutman, a cochair of the Hosanna Bench by the Road Project, told the assembled crowd:

> As we gather here today under a sunlit sky, and as we stand upon this hallowed ground, we commemorate the lives of Hinsonville's nineteenth-century African American residents: farmers, artisans, minister and missionaries; mothers, daughters, fathers and sons, all of whom came together to establish a bucolic community I which this church next to us, the Hosanna African Union Methodist Protestant Church, would serve as its heart, its soul, and its spiritual center. Together, we all have been working to commemorate a site in which Hinsonville's residents' lives can be contemplated, reflected upon, and cherished, by community members and members alike.[309]

The history and legacy of Hosanna Church are rich. From helping train ministers and burying heroes of the Civil War to hosting abolitionist speakers and being a part of the Underground Railroad, Hosanna will always be remembered as playing a major role in the life and community of southern Chester County.

Ralston Amos, an Underground Railroad agent and a founding trustee of Hosanna, wanted to receive more formal training for the ministry. Ralston was an itinerant preacher and served as the lay preacher for Hosanna when needed. Since community members took part in the preaching and pastoral work, as opposed to a minister who was assigned to the church, there was greater community involvement. This proved helpful when it came time to constructing the church and, later, the institution that would become known as Lincoln University.[310] To accomplish this, Amos

Hosanna Church was the location of the sixteenth bench placement by the Toni Morrison Society's Bench by the Road Project. *Author's collection.*

reached out to Reverend John Miller Dickey, who was the pastor of the Oxford Presbyterian Church. In the next chapter, we will discover how this quest for theological knowledge developed into the founding of the first degree-granting historically Black university.

PURSUIT OF A HIGHER EDUCATION AND THE FOUNDING OF LINCOLN UNIVERSITY

~

LINCOLN UNIVERSITY

Lincoln University is six miles from the author's home. The author received his Master of Human Services (MHS) degree from Lincoln University (LU '98). What began as a perceived need to provide education for Black people and have them, if willing, be sent to Africa as missionaries changed after the Civil War.

With the end of the Civil War, the need to educate free Black people was tremendous. It was at that time that Lincoln University changed course and began providing education without a focus on sending missionaries to Africa; rather, they focused on sending well-trained and educated Black people into local communities and beyond.

Lincoln University
1570 Baltimore Pike
Lincoln University, PA 19352
484-365-8000
www.lincoln.edu

~

REVEREND JOHN MILLER DICKEY
AND JAMES RALSTON AMOS

Reverend John Miller Dickey and the Hinsonville community, led by Ralston and Thomas Amos, founded the Ashmun Institute. *Courtesy of the Chester County History Center.*

James Ralston Amos (he went by Ralston) lived across the street from the Hosanna Meeting House and often preached there. He was also an itinerant preacher and traveled in the area to speak and serve at other African Methodist churches. Many of the Black itinerant preachers of that period were literate but had limited theological training—nor did that have much biblical knowledge. In spite of those shortcomings, Ralston was willing to travel in order to bring the gospel to as many people as he could. Still, there was a nagging thought in Ralston's mind, and that was the need for respectability. With that thought in mind, Ralston reached out to Reverend John Miller Dickey, the pastor of the Oxford Presbyterian Church in Oxford, Pennsylvania.[311]

Dickey became the pastor of the Oxford Presbyterian Church after spending time there as a missionary and preaching to the enslaved in Georgia. Dickey's wife, Sarah Emlen Cresson, was a Quaker who had, along with her family, practiced benevolence and humanitarianism while a member of the Society of Friends in Philadelphia.[312] Sarah brought that mindset with her as she served alongside her husband.

Reverend Dickey tried to place Ralston at Princeton Theological Seminary, Dickey's alma mater, but that did not work. He then tried to place Ralston in a Presbyterian Synod of Philadelphia religious academy. Due to Ralston being Black, neither attempt was successful.[313]

Realizing Ralston was sincere about his desire to receive theological training, Dickey offered to meet with him in his study at the Oxford Presbyterian Church. In order to take advantage of an-hour-a-day training for three or four days a week, Ralston would walk four miles one way from Hinsonville to Oxford and then return by the same route.[314]

Prior to beginning his four-mile trek to meet with Reverend Dickey, Ralston would stop at a stone to sit and read his Bible and pray for inspiration for that day's time with Reverend Dickey. Horace Mann Bond "captures the nearly forgotten story of the unique place of Amos's prayer stone in Lincoln's history." He wrote:

The Oxford Presbyterian Church as it looked around 1860. Ralston Amos would walk four miles one way to be tutored here by Reverend Dickey. *Courtesy of the Chester County History Center.*

The very first legend of Lincoln University relates that Amos, then living with his widowed mother in a house close by the African Union Methodist Protestant Church, walked each day the four miles to and from Oxford for an hour's instruction in the pastor's study. At the beginning of his walk, he would stop in a grove, a hundred yards from his house, later the site of Ashmun Hall, to spend a period in his daily devotions of Bible reading and prayer. He knelt at a certain stone that provided a convenient altar. Four years later, when Ashmun Hall was being built on the same site, he noted that the stone of his prayers had been placed in the foundation of the edifice.[315]

Initially Reverend Dickey was glad to assist Ralston with his pursuit of theological training and a better knowledge of Christian doctrine. Dickey quickly realized that he simply did not have time to devote to this endeavor. Aside from being the senior pastor of the Oxford Presbyterian Church, he also had responsibilities that came with founding the Oxford Female Seminary.[316]

After those failed attempts to place Ralston in established educational institutions and realizing he no longer had time to provide personal tutoring, Dickey was impressed with Ralston's desire to learn and decided it might be time to establish an educational institution that would educate Black people. Dickey thought that once trained—and if willing—graduates could be sent to Africa as missionaries to spread the gospel.

THE FOUNDING OF LINCOLN UNIVERSITY

Dr. Ernest "Ernie" C. Levister graduated from Lincoln University (LU '58). He was a Lincoln University trustee, the great-grandson of Thomas Henry Amos (LU 1859) and the great-grandnephew of James Ralston Amos (LU 1859), or, as Ernie preferred, "Ralston."

Ernie and the author have had a number of Zoom meetings to discuss the topics of this book. During one such Zoom call, Ernie and the author were discussing who founded Lincoln University. The answer Ernie gave was profound: "Lincoln University was cofounded by Reverend John Miller Dickey and the Hinsonville Community, led by Ralston Amos and his brother Thomas."[317]

KEY EVENTS IN THE FOUNDING OF LINCOLN UNIVERSITY

1. Ralston Amos reached out to Reverend Dickey in order to receive theological training.
2. Reverend Dickey was unable to place Ralston in White educational institutions.
3. Reverend Dickey offered to tutor Ralston.
4. Due to time constraints, Reverend Dickey decided it might be time to consider an educational institution specifically for Black people.
5. The initial Hinsonville property is purchased by Reverend Dickey. This was the site of the first structure of what would become Lincoln University.
6. Ralston, utilizing his experience as an itinerant preacher, went on the road to help fundraise and increase awareness of the Lincoln University project.
7. Hinsonville residents assisted with the construction of Ashmun Hall, the first building of Lincoln University.
8. A Hinsonville resident, Samuel Glasgow, provided the bricks from his brickyard for the construction of Ashmun Hall.
9. The Hosanna Meeting House Ladies' Auxiliary Society provided meals for construction workers.
10. The Hosanna Meeting House Ladies' Auxiliary Society held weekly fundraisers for Ashmun Hall.

11. Ralston Amos not only helped with the construction of Ashmun Hall, but he also became the superintendent of Ashmun Hall.
12. Ralston went into personal debt in order to provide funding for the construction of Ashmun Hall.
13. The Presbytery of New Castle approved plans for the Ashmun Institute.
14. The Commonwealth of Pennsylvania granted the charter for the Ashmun Institute.
15. Hinsonville residents provided room and board for those students who needed it prior to dorms being built.
16. Hinsonville residents sold their property to the university as the school expanded, and the Hinsonville Community disappeared.
17. Upon its completion, Amos Hall was named after the two Amos brothers, Ralston and Thomas, who led the community of Hinsonville to found the Ashmun Insitute and build Ashmun Hall.

When Emory Hinson (for whom the town of Hinsonville was named) died, his estate sold off his land holdings. John Powell purchased thirty acres of the land. Wanting to begin work on the new school, Reverend Dickey asked Powell if he would be willing to sell those acres to Dickey, and Powell agreed to do so. Dickey purchased the thirty-acre parcel of land for $1,250.[318] This parcel of land, once owned by Emory Hinson, the first resident of Hinsonville, became the cornerstone of what would become known as Lincoln University.

Dickey, who had tutored Ralston, asked Ralston if he would be willing to "go on the road" to fundraise and inform people of the upcoming project. Ralston's experience as an itinerant preacher made this task perfect for him. Ralston had come to know many Black people at various churches and in many communities during his travels. Not only could he ask for donations, but he could also explain the exciting news that an educational institution was being proposed where Black people could receive an education.

The construction of Ashmun Hall, the first building constructed on the John Powell/Emory Hinson property, involved most of the Hinsonville residents. They had seen how, working together, they were able to construct the Hosanna Meeting House. The residents donated their time and money to see Ashmun Hall come to fruition.

Samuel Glasgow was known in the area for his brickyard. His bricks were used by the Hinsonville residents in the construction of Ashmun Hall and other buildings after that.[319] Ralston and his brother Thomas were trustees of both Hinsonville and Hosanna. They were well liked and respected. Because of this, they were able to lead the residents of Hinsonville to build Ashmun Hall.

One time, Ralston was on his way to see how the construction of Ashmun Hall was progressing and went to his "stone altar" to pray a prayer of thanksgiving, only to discover that his altar was missing. After doing some research, he discovered his stone was part of the foundation of the new building. Along with the "altar stone" being apart of the foundation, there was also a unique cornerstone—it was made from a tombstone. "On the back was carved a hand pointing toward heaven. On the front was engraved the name of the school, the date and motto, 'The night is far spent, the day is at hand.' The new building faced due-east, toward the rising sun."[320]

The Ladies' Auxiliary Society from the Hosanna Meeting House provided meals for the construction workers who were building Ashmun Hall. Along with providing meals, the society also held weekly fundraisers to provide financial assistance for the Ashmun project.

Once Ashmun Hall was completed, Ralston Amos became the superintendent of the building. Ralston was dedicated to seeing an educational institution for Black people come to fruition, as evidenced by his willingness to go into significant personal debt.[321]

As Lincoln University continued to expand, more Hinsonville residents sold their land to the university. Major expansion of the university did not begin until after the Civil War. This was when the need for teachers became apparent, as there were more than 4 million freed enslaved people in dire need of an education. Lincoln began to receive federal grants to help with the growth of the school. With that grant money, the university grew, and Hinsonville continued to shrink.

Charles Thomas Glasgow used to have a country store across the way from Hosanna Meeting House. He died in 1868, and the university quickly bought Glasgow's property. Another store was purchased in 1871. Today, Mary Dod Brown Chapel sits on the site of Elias P. Draper's store.

Ralston and Thomas Amos were members of the first graduating class of the Ashmun Institute. Both brothers went to Liberia to serve as missionaries. Ralston's health continued to worsen while he was in Liberia, and finally, in 1864, he returned home for good. It was only a short time later that he passed away at the age of thirty-nine.[322]

Left: Elias P. Draper sold his store and property to Lincoln University. Today, the Mary Dod Chapel sits on the site of Draper's store. *Courtesy of the Chester County History Center.*

Right: Sarah Hunter Amos, the widow of Thomas Amos, built Amos House, which served as a lodging and dining hall for Lincoln students. *Author's collection.*

Thomas was able to stay in Liberia a little while longer. While he was the pastor of the Presbyterian Church in Monrovia, one of the parishioners was Daniel B. Warner, the president of Liberia.[323] In 1869, while he was still in Liberia, Thomas died at the age of forty-three.

The Ashmun Institute was cofounded by Reverend John Miller Dickey and the Hinsonville community, led by Ralston and Thomas Amos. Unfortunately, neither brother lived long enough to see the long-term results their efforts produced. However, their names live on at Lincoln University. There are two buildings with the Amos name: Amos Hall (named after the Amos brothers) and Amos House (named after Sarah Hunter Amos, Thomas Amos's wife). Amos descendants have been Lincoln students, trustees and faculty members.

The plaque on the outside of the Amos House reads:

Amos House. In memory of Sarah Hunter Amos, widow of Thomas Henry Amos who was a graduate of the first class of Ashmun Institute (later renamed Lincoln University), ordained as a Presbyterian minister and served in Moravia, Liberia, as the first Black Presbyterian missionary from 1859–1870. After her husband's death, she returned to America and built this house to serve as lodging facilities and dining hall for Lincoln students and worked untiringly for them from 1871–1903. Their son, the late Reverend Thomas Hunter Amos, class of 1897, deeded this house to Lincoln University in 1926 with request it be held as a memorial in honor of this courageous and resourceful woman.

At this time, the Amos House is in need of major restoration. The building is not in use at this time and is not open to the public.

Ashmun Institute/Lincoln University

The Ashmun Institute was named after Jehudi Ashmun, who helped found Liberia. Ashmun was involved with the American Colonization Society, whose members "supported sending free Blacks and emancipated slaves there, rather than advocate for granting them full rights as American citizens."[324] After President Abraham Lincoln was assassinated, the school was renamed Lincoln University.

Reverend Dickey supported the American Colonization Society and wanted to establish an educational institution that could train Black men to go to Africa to serve as missionaries. The Presbytery of New Castle reviewed and endorsed the establishment of "an institution to be called Ashmun Institute, for the scientific, classical, and theological education of colored youth of the male sex." This occurred in October 1853.[325] It was during the next year, on April 29, 1854, that the Commonwealth of Pennsylvania granted a charter to Ashmun Institute, making "it the nation's first degree-granting historically Black college or university (NBCU)."[326]

The education that was provided in the university's early years had a strong Presbyterian presence which made sense seeing where the New Castle Presbytery approved Reverend Dickey's initial application. Many of the early graduates entered the missionary field and headed to Africa. Those who did not become missionaries became Methodist, Baptist or Presbyterian ministers. Christianity was at the forefront of the university. There was morning and evening chapel, as well as a Sunday service. Students were accepted to the school, even if they had no background in Christianity or biblical teachings. Those students quickly learned about both, as the Bible served as one of the school's major textbooks.[327]

The curriculum in the early days of Ashmun/Lincoln University was divided into three parts:

> *Preparatory, academic, and theological. The Preparatory Department began as a three-year program, teaching Latin and Greek grammar and English at the level typical of public high schools. Hen slaves were freed and had greater access to secondary education, the preparatory program was condensed into a one-year program. The Academic Department, a four-year higher education program, taught biblical and classical studies, science, and philosophy. The Theological Department was a three-year program that awarded students the degree of bachelor of sacred theology (BST).*[328]

To prevent the spread of antislavery texts, southern lawmakers barred the teaching of the enslaved and even free Black people.[329] These antiliteracy laws impacted the enslaved, freedmen and, often, free Black people. "Between 1740 and 1834, Alabama, Georgia, Louisiana, Mississippi, North and South Carolina, and Virginia all passed anti-literacy laws." Significant anti-Black laws included:

1829, Georgia: Prohibited teaching Black people to read, punishable by fines and imprisonment.

1832, Alabama and Virginia: Prohibited White people from teaching Black people to read or write, punishable by fines and floggings.

1833, Georgia: Prohibited Black people from working in reading or writing jobs (via an employment law) and prohibited the teaching of Black people, punishable by fines and whippings (via an antiliteracy law).

1847, Missouri: Prohibited the assembling or teaching of the enslaved.

The United States is the only country known to have had antiliteracy laws.[330]

The Southern states knew literacy was a key the enslaved could use on their quest for freedom, and that is why slaveowners were adamant they never learn to read or write. With the end of the Civil War and the freeing of over 4 million enslaved people, the need for and desire by both freed people and free people for education increased.

The end of the Civil War was a watershed moment in the history of the Ashmun Institute. The enlaved were set free, and the Union army had won the Civil War. The importance of the American Colonization Society disappeared. Ashmun was low on funds and low on enrolled students until

Lincoln University's sign. *Author's collection.*

then. Suddenly, there were free Black people who needed to be educated for life at home—not abroad. Freed people needed to be educated, along with war veterans. It was unrealistic to think that Lincoln University could meet the needs of so many freed people desiring to learn to read and write. This is why the school began training teachers to go into communities to teach freed people.

It was at this time that Lincoln University changed course and began providing education with the focus not on sending missionaries to Africa but on sending well-trained and educated Black people into local communities and beyond. The importance of being able to provide an education for the 4 million recently freed people was recognized. Seeing that so many freed people were unable to read or write, attending a university such as Lincoln was out of the question. However, the need for teachers to go into communities to teach freed people the basics of reading and writing was of utmost importance. The federal government recognized Lincoln could help meet that need and provided the school with grant money to expand its land holdings and build new structures.

Amos Hall, which has frieze of Abraham Lincoln and Ralston Amos, is currently undergoing renovations. *Author's collection.*

Change was taking place. The American Colonization Society was no longer relevant, and the Underground Railroad was no longer needed. Former Underground Railroad stationmasters wanted to continue providing assistance to the then-freed people. One way they achieved this goal was by joining forces with the Freedmen's Aid Society. This society was formed during the Civil War, and its goal was to provide teachers with housing in the South so they could educate freed Black people and their children.[331]

> *During its early years, Lincoln was colloquially known as "the Black Princeton," due to its Princeton University–educated founder and early faculty, rigorous classical curriculum, ties to the Presbyterian Church and its similarities in colors and mascots. (Princeton's colors: orange and black; Lincoln's colors: orange and blue; Princeton's mascot: the tiger; Lincoln's mascot: the lion).[332]*

The residents of Hinsonville, led by Ralston and Thomas Amos, came together to help with the construction of Ashmun Hall, the beginning of what was to become Ashmun Institute. To honor the contribution the two Amos brothers made to the founding of Ashmun Institute, both on their own and in their leadership roles among the Hinsonville community, a building was built and dedicated to them: Amos Hall. Over the entrance to the hall is a friese. On the one side, there is the only known image of Ralston Amos, and on the other side is an image of President Abraham Lincoln.

Amos Hall is currently undergoing extensive renovations. This is a welcome sight, as the building holds such historic significance.

LINCOLN UNIVERSITY TODAY

Founded in 1854:

> *The Lincoln University (PA) is the FIRST of four Lincoln Universities in the world and is the nation's FIRST degree-granting historically Black college of university (HBCU). The university combines the elements of a liberal arts and science-based undergraduate curriculum, along with select graduate programs to meet the needs of those living in a highly technological and global society. Today, Lincoln, which enrolls a diverse student body of approximately 2,000 men and women, possesses an international reputation for preparing and producing world class leaders, such as Thurgood Marshall,*

LINCOLN UNIVERSITY

Chartered as Ashmun Institute,
April 29, 1854. Founded by Rev.
John Miller Dickey for the purpose of providing liberal higher
education for people of African
ancestry in America. In 1866, it
became Lincoln University, inter-
racial and international.

This marker acknowledges the oldest degree-granting historically Black university in the country. *Courtesy of the Pennsylvania Historic and Museum.*

the FIRST African American U.S. Supreme Court justice; Lillian Fishburne, the FIRST African American woman promoted to rear admiral in the U.S. Navy; Langston Hughes, the noted poet; Kwame Nkrumah, the FIRST president of Ghana; Nnamdi Azikiwe, the FIRST president of Nigeria; and a myriad of others.[333] (See appendix A for more FIRSTs.)

The director of Alumni Relations Rita Dibble uses the concept of being first to challenge newly arriving students to Lincoln University. According to Dibble, "the challenge to our students is to define the areas in which [they are] the first. They walk in here and they are told about Langston Hughes and Thurgood Marshall. We ask them, 'How will you be the first?'"[334]

For many of the new students, they are already a first. According to communications director Eric Webb, "A great portion of our students are first-generation college students or first in their high school class. It's a nice mix of people that are first in their class, first in their family, and we treat you first."[335]

One of the firsts was Dr. Horace Mann Bond, the first Black president of Lincoln University. Dr. Bond developed a personal relationship with Dr. Albert C. Barnes, the founder of the Barnes Foundation, and this turned into an institutional relationship as well. For further information, see appendix B.

Throughout its history, Lincoln University has made an impact on its students and the global community. The motto of the university, "If the Son shall make you free, ye shall be free indeed," stressed the importance of freed people obtaining an education. "Slaves and sometimes free Blacks had been denied—by custom and often by law—the right to a formal education, and they believed access to the word to be an essential element of freedom, as well as a practical means of self-advancement. Literacy would enable them to crack the secret code White men had used to enslave them."[336]

❧ ❧ ❧

Ralston and Thomas Amos moved to Hinsonville and helped develop the community. They also helped to build the Hosanna Church, which would go on to host such speakers as Frederick Douglass and Sojourner Truth. Hosanna would host Oxford Clarkson Anti-Slavery Society meetings and would be an active participant in the Underground Railroad.

Lincoln University was cofounded by Reverend John Miller Dickey, and the Hinsonville community, led by Ralston Amos and his brother Thomas Henry, built it. Together, these two brothers helped bring freedom to many people during their lives and well after their deaths. Because of their work in cofounding Lincoln University, Black people could come to be trained as teachers and go forth into their communities, bringing freedom to free people who needed the freedom of literacy, which had been denied by their slave owners and others who worked to keep the Black community oppressed and illiterate. Their legacy lives on today.

Appendix A

HISTORY OF
LINCOLN UNIVERSITY FIRSTS

(International firsts and impact are in italics.)[337]

1854

Established as the nation's first degree-granting historically black college and university (HBCU).

1859

The first graduate of Lincoln University, then the Ashmun Institute, James Ralston Amos.

1865

Among the first Congressional Medal of Honor recipients was U.S. Civil War veteran Christian Fleetwood, class of 1860.

1874

The first Black person to graduate from Yale School of Divinity, James William Morris, class of 1871.

1875

The first Black Yale Divinity student and the first Black person to receive a bachelor of divinity degree after completing the full three-year theological program at Yale Divinity School, Samuel (Solomon) Melvin Coles, class of 1872.

1879

The first president and founder of Livingstone College (North Carolina), Joseph Charles Price, PhD, class of 1879.

1884

The first alumni publication for a U.S. college. Its staff also included abolitionist, orator and educator Frederick Douglass as an early writer.

1888

The first Black person to graduate from the University of Pennsylvania Law School, Aaron Albert Mossell, class of 1855.

1896

The first president of South Carolina State University, Thomas Ezekiel Miller, class of 1872.

1903

Founder of Albany State University (Georgia), Joseph Winthrop Holley, class of 1900.

1910

The first Black person elected to the Pennsylvania General Assembly, Harry W. Bass, class of 1886.

1920

The first registered Black architect in Georgia and the founder of the nation's first Black architecture firm, Taylor and Persley (with his partner, Robert Taylor), Louis H. Persley, class of 1908.

The first Black person to receive a doctorate in psychology and the father of Black psychology, Francis Cecil Sumner, class of 1915.

The first Black person to serve in the New Jersey legislature, Walter G. Alexander, class of 1899.

1921

The first African American National Football League coach (Akron Pros), Fritz Pollard, the former coach of the Lincoln University football team (1918–20 season).

1932

The first African American to earn both a master's degree (1929, Harvard University) and doctorate (Columbia University), Hildrus A. Poindexter, class of 1924. He was also the first Black person to be an internationally recognized authority on tropical diseases.

1939

First president of Fort Valley State University (Georgia), Horace Mann Bond, PhD, class of 1923.

1945

The eighth president and first Black president of Lincoln University, Horace Mann Bond, class of 1923.

1947

The first Black Pennsylvania judge (Philadelphia Municipal Court), Herbert E. Millen, class of 1910.

The first president of Texas Southern University, Dr. R. O'Hara Lanier, class of 1941.

1950

The first Black university affiliated with the College Entrance Examinations Board.

1951

The founder of Kwame Nkrumah University of Science and Technology (Ghana), Kwame Nkrumah, class of 1939.

1953

The first female graduate of Lincoln University, Ruth Fales, class of 1953.

1955

The first Black female graduate of Lincoln University, Gladys W. Walls, class of 1955.

The founder of the University of Nigeria, Nnamdi Azikiwe, class of 1930.

1958

The first Black U.S. congressman for Pennsylvania, Robert N.C. Nix Sr., class of 1928.

1960

The first president of Ghana, Kwame Nkrumah, class of 1939.

1962

The first Black U.S. postal inspector, Charles A. Preston Jr., class of 1950.

1963

The first group of Peace Corps trainees arrived on Lincoln's campus for their training session. Ironically, the Peace Corps was modeled after Crossroads Africa, an organization founded by Reverend James Robinson, class of 1935, in 1957.

The first president of Nigeria, Nnamdi Azikiwe, class of 1930.

The first Black faculty member at the University of Pennsylvania, William Fontaine, class of 1930.

1967

The first Black associate justice of the United States Supreme Court, Justice Thurgood Marshall, class of 1930.

1968

The first tenured Black faculty member at Harvard University, Martin L. Kilson Jr., PhD, class of 1953.

The first Black bishop of the United Methodist Church, Bishop Roy C. Nichols, class of 1941.

1969

The first Black dean in the School of Arts at California State Polytechnic University (Pomona), James Bell, class of 1952.

1970

The first Black assistant to California State Polytechnic University, Pomona's vice-president of academic affairs James Bell, class of 1952.

1972

The first Black vice-president of the California State University System, James Bell, class of 1952.

The first Black tenured professor at the University of Pennsylvania School of Medicine, Edward S. Cooper, MD, class of 1946.

1975

The first Black mayor of Ann Arbor, Michigan, Albert Wheeler, class of 1936.

1984

The first Black mayor of Atlantic City, New Jersey, James L. Usry, class of 1946.

1985

The first Black person to have a federal building, a courthouse, dedicated in his honor, Clarence Mitchell Jr., class of 1932. He was a civil rights activist and longtime lobbyist for the National Association for the Advancement of Colored People (NAACP). The Baltimore, Maryland courthouse on the west side of Calvert Street bears his name.

1987

The first alumna elected to the Lincoln University Board of Trustees by the alumni association, Delores Kirby Coleman, class of 1972.

The first female president of Lincoln University, Niara Sudarkasa, PhD.

1990

Namibia's first independent government cabinet had at least six Lincoln University graduates in it.

1992

The first Black president of the American Heart Association, Edward C. Cooper, MD, class of 1946.

1994

The first Black chief justice of the Tennessee Supreme Court, A.A. Birch Jr., class of 1952.

1995

The rector of the Polytechnic of Namibia, Tjama Tjivikua, PhD, class of 1983.

1997

The first Black associate justice of the Massachusetts Supreme Judicial Court, Roderick L. Ireland, class of 1966.

1998

The first Black female United States Navy rear admiral, Lilliam Fishburn, class of 1971.

1999–2003

The first woman to chair Lincoln University's board of trustees, Adrienne G. Rhone, class of 1976.

Early 2000s

The first Black dean of the University of Pretoria after the dismantling of apartheid, Sibusio Vil-Nkomo, PhD, class of 1981.

2002–3

The first American university to have two alumni honored with commemorative, first-class United States postage stamps: poet Langston Hughes, January 2002; and United States Supreme Court justice Thurgood Marshall, February 2003.

2005

Appointed deputy governor of the South African Reserve Bank, Renosi Mokate, class of 1981.

2007

The first minority president of the American Association for Marriage and Family Therapy, Scott Johnson, PhD, class of 1973.

2009–10

The first Black president and then–first Black chairman of the board of directors for the United States Distance Learning Association, E. Reggie Smith III, PhD, class of 1992.

2010

Appointed executive director of the World Bank Group, Renosi Mokate, class of 1981.

Appointed executive dean of the Graduate School of Business Leadership at the University of South Africa, Renosi Mokate, class of 1981.

2015

The first female prime minister of Namibia, Saara Kuugongelwa, class of 1994.

The first alumna president of a college or university, the president of California State Polytechnic University (Pomona) Soraya Coley, class of 1972.

Lincoln University became the first HBCU to charter a "hall" or pre-law society chapter (for undergraduates) of Phi Delta Phi International Legal Honor Society. "Lincoln University Hall" was organized and founded by students, Gionelly Mills (class of 1918) and Shereka Ellington (class of 1918).

The youngest recipient of a doctorate from Delaware State University, Jalaal A. Hayes, PhD, class of 2011 (age twenty-two).

2016

The first Black person to lead Metro Nashville Schools, Shawn Joseph, class of 1996.

The first female Philadelphia prisons commissioner, Blanche Carney, class of 1992.

2017

The first female Lincoln University alumna selected as the president of the university, Brenda A. Allen, class of 1981.

The first Black female lieutenant governor of New Jersey, the Honorable Sheila Y. Oliver, class of 1974.

2020

The first Black female speaker of the New Jersey General Assembly, the Honorable Sheila Y. Oliver, class of 1974.

The largest single gift in Lincoln's history: MacKenzie Scott donated $20 million to Lincoln University.

Appendix B

ALBERT BARNES AND THE BARNES FOUNDATION AND ARBORETUM

WHO WAS ALBERT BARNES?

Albert Barnes (1872–1951) grew up in the poor section of Philadelphia. There, he was exposed to "overcrowded neighborhoods, bad housing, deplorable health and horrible working conditions."[338] Barnes reported one of his most important life events was "when he first heard Black spirituals sung at a camp meeting his mother had taken him to as a young child."[339] Remembering those songs, he later called them "the greatest art America has produced," representing "the collective grief and aspirations of their race."[340]

Dr. Barnes cared about Black Americans as evidenced by the following:

1. He started a scholarship program for young Black Americans who wanted to study the arts, including painting, music and writing.
2. He promoted works of Black Americans through programs at the Barnes.
3. He collected artwork by Black artist Horace Pippin.
4. He was a member of the Association for the Study of Negro Life and History.
5. He was involved with the New Negro Movement (also called the Harlem Renaissance).
6. At his Argyrol Factory, Barnes employed twelve Black men.
7. Employees were provided with a lifelong pension from Barnes.

8. The widows of the employees were also given a lifelong pension.
9. Barnes frequently attended NAACP dinners.
10. Black churches often benefitted from his generosity.
11. Black students received scholarships from Barnes.
12. The Barnes Foundation's collection of African objects was the first "fine art" collection in the United States.[341]

Barnes was aware of social injustices and took the time to try to right them. He knew of a Black medical student who could obtain a residency in the mostly White hospitals in America. Barnes came up with a solution: he obtained a residency for the medical student at a hospital in Paris. Another time, there was a Black musician who wanted to study the organ. Unable to find anyone willing to work with him, Barnes stepped in and paid for the young musician to study with a world-renowned organist in Paris.[342]

Thanks to Barnes, his employees could enjoy a six-hour workday. The other two hours were provided as learning opportunities for employees. Many of his employees were either uneducated or undereducated. Having grown up in poverty and with a limited education, Barnes wanted to provide opportunities for his employees to grow in their education and knowledge. During his lectures and teachings, Barnes covered subjects ranging from racial injustice and economic hardships to psychology, which provided the groundwork for his foundation courses later in his career.

BARNES FOUNDATION AND LINCOLN UNIVERSITY:

In 1946, Dr. Albert Barnes, the founder and president of the Barnes Foundation, and Dr. Horace Mann Bond, the first Black president of Lincoln University, were at the same funeral, and both gave eulogies. After the funeral, the two men had the opportunity to talk and get to know each other. This may have been an accidental meeting, "but the alliance of their two institutions was by choice. In 1950...Dr. Barnes amended the Indenture of Trust for the Barnes Foundation to provide that Lincoln University would eventually nominate four of the five trustees of that foundation."[343] This decision by Barnes shook the art world and the higher educational world as well. There were so many who could not believe that a little school out in the middle of the country would suddenly gain control of a world-famous and wealthy foundation.

At the time, the Barnes Foundation was located in Merion, Pennsylvania. While at Lincoln, Dr. Ernest Levister (LU '58) remembered hearing that Lincoln students would go to the Barnes Foundation for tours and lectures. Joseph Hill was the dean of the college and a professor of general literature. His classes in 1951, 1952 and 1953 went to the Barnes. Joseph Hill was the first Black professors at Lincoln.[344]

There was much controversy when the Indenture of Trust for the Barnes Foundation was overturned in 2004. Under the original Indenture of Trust, Lincoln would fill four out of the five trustee positions, giving Lincoln 80 percent control. Under the new Indenture of Trust, Lincoln would fill five out of the fifteen trustee positions, giving Lincoln only 33 percent control. This new agreement effectively diluted Lincoln's influence.

Merion, Pennsylvania, in Lower Merion Township was chosen by Dr. Barnes as the place to house his art collection and the Barnes Foundation. Dr. Barnes's will prohibited the art collection from ever being moved from the Lower Merion site. He envisioned and ran the foundation as a school for art education and appreciation. He never saw it as a museum open to the general public. However, it appears that the City of Philadelphia had other plans and wanted the collection moved to create a museum that would attract many tourists.[345]

In 2009, a documentary directed by Don Argott, *The Art of the Steal*, was released. Its subject was the breaking of Dr. Albert Barnes's will and moving his art collection to the city of Philadelphia. In his review of the film, Roger Ebert of the *Chicago Sun-Times* wrote:

> *It is perfectly clear exactly what Barnes specified in his will. It was drawn up by the best legal minds. It is clear that what happened to his collection was against his wishes. It is clear that the city fathers acted in obviation of those wishes and were upheld in a court of appeals. What is finally clear: It doesn't matter a damn what your will says if you have $25 billion and politicians and the establishment want it.*[346]

BARNES ARBORETUM AT ST. JOSEPH'S UNIVERSITY

While Dr. Albert C. Barnes was building his art collection and forming the Barnes Foundation, his wife, Laura Leggett Barnes, worked on the arboretum that had been started by the previous owner of the Merion, Pennsylvania property, Captain Joseph Lapsley Wilson. He had been collecting various specimens of trees. The Barnes couple kept Wilson on as the director of the arboretum. Laura Barnes continued collecting many plants, some of which were quite rare. In 1940, she started a horticultural school.[347]

The Barnes Foundation partnered with St. Joseph's University in 2018. While the Barnes Foundation oversees the arboretum, its day-to-day operations and grounds maintenance are now overseen by St. Joseph's University. William Rein, the assistant director of the Living Collections and Horticultural Programs–Barnes Arboretum at St. Joseph's University, said the program the university offers is similar to the Horticulture Certificate Program that was started under Laura Barnes. According to Rein:

> *The program operates with a structure similar to that which existed in Laura Barnes' time—three years, one full day of classes per week each year, with basic botanical and related science courses and plant ID courses, with multiple landscape design courses in the second and third years, but over the years, the course subjects have grown to include plant pathology, weed science, etc. And we still include one course in Barnes art (Element of Art) as well as history of landscape architecture and a landscape analysis course (previously titled "Garden Appreciation") that encourages observation of plants in the arboretum's living collections through the seasons.*[348]

NOTES

Chapter 1

1. Wikipedia, "History of Slavery."
2. Kashatus, *Just Over the Line*, 8.
3. Wikipedia, "History of Slavery."
4. Kashatus, *Just Over the Line*, 88–91.
5. Russo and Russo, *Hinsonville*, 11.
6. Ecenbarger, *Walkin' the Line*, 15.
7. Ibid.
8. Ibid.
9. Kashatus, *Just Over the Line*, 7.
10. Landefeld, *Changing Boundaries*, 83.
11. Nathan, *East of the Mason-Dixon*, 10.
12. Ecenbarger, *Walkin' the Line*, 15.
13. Ibid., 13.
14. Ibid., 15.
15. Kashatus, *Just Over the Line*, 10.
16. Switala, *Underground Railroad*, 7.
17. Kashatus, *Just Over the Line*, 10.
18. Turner, "Abolition of Slavery," 136.
19. Kashatus, *Just Over the Line*, 15.
20. Wikipedia, "History of Slavery."
21. Turner, "Abolition of Slavery," 136.

22. Ibid., 129.
23. American History Central Online, "Act of 1793."
24. Ibid.
25. American History Central Online, "Act of 1793 Facts."
26. Leslie, "Pennsylvania Fugitive Slave Act," 430.
27. Ibid., 429.
28. American History Central Online, "Act of 1793 Facts."
29. American History Central Online, "Act of 1850."
30. American History Central Online, "Act of 1850 Facts."
31. Ibid.
32. American History Central Online, "Act of 1850."
33. Maddox, *Parker Sisters*, 4.
34. Switala, *Underground Railroad*, 10.

Chapter 2

35. Bordewich, *Bound for Canaan*, 5.
36. Turner, "Underground Railroad," 310.
37. Kashatus, *Just Over the Line*, 2.
38. Bond, *Education for Freedom*, 196.
39. Taylor, *Trackless Trail*, 4.
40. Smedley, *History of the Underground Railroad*, 34.
41. Kashatus, *Just Over the Line*, 51.
42. Ecenbarger, *Walkin' the Line*, 105.
43. Hoffman, "Kennett's Underground Railroad."
44. Kashatus, *Just Over the Line*, 92.
45. Murray, *Proud Shoes*, 95.
46. Schultz, "Hosanna Church."
47. Murray, *Proud Shoes*, 96.
48. Smedley, *History of the Underground Railroad*, 32.
49. *Bulletin for the 150ᵗʰ Anniversary*, 4.
50. Kashatus, *Just Over the Line*, 50–51.
51. Calarco, *People of the Underground Railroad*, 125.
52. Gara, "Friends and Underground Railroad," 8–9.
53. Kashatus and Stavenski, *Traveling the Eastern Line*, 12.
54. Murray, *Proud Shoes*, 83.
55. Taylor, *Trackless Trail Leads On*, 14.
56. Smedley, *History of the Underground Railroad*, 244.

57. Taylor, *Trackless Trail Leads On*, 14.
58. Kashatus and Stavenski, *Traveling the Eastern Line*, 12.
59. Calarco, *People of the Underground Railroad*, 125.
60. *Bulletin for the 150th Anniversary*, 4.
61. Taylor, *Trackless Trail*, 4.
62. Smedley, *History of the Underground Railroad*, 241.
63. *Bulletin for the 150th Anniversary*, 4.
64. Ibid.
65. Blockson, *Hippocrene Guide*, 99.
66. *Bulletin for the 150th Anniversary*, 4.
67. *Kennett News and Advertiser*, February 18, 1942.
68. Taylor, *Trackless Trail*, 7.
69. Kashatus and Stavenski, *Traveling the Eastern Line*, 15.
70. U.S. National Park Service, "Underground Railroad—Oakdale."
71. *Bulletin for the 150th Anniversary*, 4.
72. Calarco, *People of the Underground Railroad*, 84.
73. *Bulletin for the 150th Anniversary*, 4.
74. Taylor, *Trackless Trail Leads On*, 29.
75. Wikipedia, "Bartholomew Fussell."
76. *Kennett News and Advertiser*, February 18, 1942.
77. Calarco, *People of the Underground Railroad*, 120.
78. *Kennett News and Advertiser*, February 18, 1942.
79. Ibid.
80. Calarco, *People of the Underground Railroad*, 120.
81. Smedley, *History of the Underground Railroad*, 313.
82. Taylor, *Trackless Trail Leads On*, 30.
83. Smedley, *History of the Underground Railroad*, 315.
84. Kopaczewski, "Christiana Riot Trial."
85. Dixon, "Civil-War Era Man."
86. *Bulletin for the 150th Anniversary*, 4.
87. Taylor, *Trackless Trail*, 20.
88. Ibid., 26.
89. James, *Potters and Potteries*, 104.
90. Smedley, *History of the Underground Railroad*, 34.
91. James, *Potter and Potteries*, 37.
92. *Bulletin for the 150th Anniversary*, 4.
93. Lucas, "Lincoln's Quakers Roots."
94. PocketSights, "Kennett Area Underground Railroad."
95. Taylor, *Trackless Trail Leads On*, 59.

96. Ibid., 56.
97. Ibid.
98. Kashatus, *Just Over the Line*, 92.
99. Taylor, *Trackless Trail Leads On*, 4.
100. Ecenbarger, *Walkin' the Line*, 103–4.
101. Calarco, *People of the Underground Railroad*, 306.
102. Taylor, *Trackless Trail*, 32–33.
103. Kashatus, *Just Over the Line*, 18.
104. Taylor, *Trackless Trail Leads On*, 4.
105. Calarco, *People of the Underground Railroad*, 309.
106. Garrison, *Amazing Women*, 46.
107. Slavery Monuments, "Harriett Tubman."
108. Taylor, *Trackless Trail*, 24.
109. Ibid.
110. Smedley, *History of the Underground Railroad*, 247–48.
111. Ibid., 251–52.
112. Kashatus and Stavenski, *Traveling the Eastern Line*, 19.
113. Ibid.
114. PocketSights, "Kennett Area Underground Railroad."
115. Ibid.
116. Kashatus and Stavenski, *Traveling the Eastern Line*, 13.
117. James, *Potter and Potteries*, 45.
118. Dugan and Sestrich, *East Linden Street*, 35–38.
119. Wiley, *Biographical and Portrait Cyclopedia*, 666.
120. Dugan and Sestrich, *East Linden Street*, 35–38.
121. Ibid., 19.
122. Ibid.
123. Ibid.
124. Smedley, *History of the Underground Railroad*, 249–50.
125. U.S. National Park Service, "Underground Railroad—Oakdale."
126. PocketSights, "Cox Residence."
127. Taylor, *Trackless Trail*, 12.
128. Wikipedia, "Bartholomew Fussell."
129. Taylor, *Trackless Trail*, 29.
130. Taylor, *Trackless Trail Leads On*, 18.

Chapter 3

131. Historical Society of Pennsylvania Online, "Pennsylvania Abolition Society."

132. Switala, *Underground Railroad*, 7–8.

133. Turner, "Abolition of Slavery," 129.

134. Turner, "First Abolition Society," 94–95.

135. Jordan, *Slavery and the Meetinghouse*, 107.

136. Bryn Mawr, "Quakers and Slavery."

137. Ohio History Central, "American Anti-Slavery Society."

138. Wikipedia, "American Anti-Slavery Society."

139. Bryn Mawr, "Quakers and Slavery."

140. Patten, *Anti-Slavery Movement*, 40.

141. Ibid., 41.

142. *Liberator* (Boston, MA), September 13, 1834.

143. Patten, *Anti-Slavery Movement*, 42.

144. Gooch, *Africa's Lands*, 5.

145. Patten, *Anti-Slavery Movement*, 43–44.

146. *Register and Examiner* (West Chester, PA), February 28, 1837.

147. *Coatesville Weekly Times*, November 21, 1837.

148. Patten, *Anti-Slavery Movement*, 50.

149. Calarco, *People of the Underground Railroad*, 83.

150. Smedley, *History of the Underground Railroad*, 248.

151. Wikipedia, "Ercildoun."

152. *Pennsylvania Freeman*, October 3, 1850.

153. Ibid.

154. Jordan, *Slavery and the Meetinghouse*, 37.

155. Ibid.

156. Patten, *Anti-Slavery Movement*, 70.

157. Nuermberger, *Free Produce Movement*, 20.

158. Taylor, *Trackless Trail Leads On*, 33.

159. Wilkinson, "Philadelphia Free Produce Attack," 308–11.

160. Lucas, "Lincoln's Quakers Roots."

161. Murray, *Proud Shoes*, 97–98.

162. Ibid.

163. Kashatus, *Just Over the Line*, 25.

164. Murray, *Proud Shoes*, 97–98.

165. Maddox, *Parker Sisters*, 34–35.

166. Ibid.

167. *Pennsylvania Freeman*, September 6, 1849.

168. Carey and Plank, *Quakers and Abolition*, 128–29.
169. ExplorePAHistory.com, "Christiana Riot Historical Marker."
170. Ibid.
171. Ibid.
172. Smedley, *History of the Underground Railroad*, 247–48.
173. Lewis, "Recollections," 315.
174. Smedley, *History of the Underground Railroad*, 252.
175. ExplorePAHistory.com, "Christiana Riot Historical Marker."
176. Rice, *Legacy Transformed*, 79.
177. Russo and Russo, *Hinsonville*, 87.
178. Kopaczewski, "Christiana Riot Trial."
179. Ibid.
180. ExplorePAHistory.com, "Christiana Riot Historical Marker."
181. Patten, *Anti-Slavery Movement*, 51.
182. Harris and Hopkins, "Resistance."
183. Ibid.
184. Ibid.
185. Rice, *Legacy Transformed*, 310.
186. Ibid., 311–12.
187. Ibid., 313.
188. Lucas, "Lincoln's Quakers Roots."
189. Pisasale, "Pathway to Freedom."
190. African American Civil War Museum, "Tradition of Watch Night."
191. Ibid.
192. American History Central Online, "Emancipation Proclamation."
193. Ibid.
194. U.S. National Archives and Records Administration, "Transcript."
195. Kashatus, *Just Over the Line*, 79.

Chapter 4

196. Densmore, "Be Ye Therefore Perfect," 30–31.
197. *Bulletin for the 150th Anniversary*, 5.
198. Densmore, "Truth for Authority."
199. *Bulletin for the 150th Anniversary*, 5.
200. Densmore, "Be Ye Therefore Perfect," 28.
201. Ibid., 28–29.
202. Ibid., 30–31.

203. Ibid., 32.
204. Ibid.
205. Ibid.
206. Ibid., 33.
207. Ibid.
208. Ibid., 35.
209. Wikipedia, "Ercildoun."
210. Densmore, "Be Ye Therefore Perfect," 38.
211. Haas, "Route to Freedom."
212. Taylor, *Trackless Trail*, 16.
213. Densmore, "Be Ye Therefore Perfect," 40.
214. Ibid., 39.
215. Ibid., 41.
216. Yarnall, "Longwood Meeting," 50–51.
217. Densmore, "Be Ye Therefore Perfect," 41–42.
218. Switala, *Underground Railroad*, 152.
219. *Bulletin for the 150th Anniversary*, 4.
220. Wahl, "Progressive Friends," 32.
221. Ibid., 19.
222. PocketSights, "Kennett Area Underground Tour."
223. *Philadelphia Record*, May 6, 1906.
224. Densmore, "Truth for Authority."
225. Kashatus and Stavenski, *Traveling the Eastern Line*, 17.
226. Taylor, *Trackless Trail*, 18.
227. Wikipedia, "Frederick Douglass."
228. Ibid.
229. Reynolds, *Mightier Than the Sword*, 116.
230. Ibid., 129–30.
231. Ibid., 118.
232. Ibid., 130.
233. Pisasale, "Pathway to Freedom."
234. Garrison, *Amazing Women*, 221.
235. Reynolds, *Mightier Than the Sword*, 130.
236. U.S. Senate, "Landmark Legislation."
237. Smedley, *History of the Underground Railroad*, 280.
238. Wikipedia, "Sojourner Truth."
239. Smedley, *History of the Underground Railroad*, 256.
240. Wikipedia, "Susan B. Anthony."
241. Ibid.

242. PocketSights, "East Linden Street."

243. Kashatus, *Just Over the Line*, 73.

244. *Bulletin for the 150th Anniversary*, 2.

245. Kashatus and Stavenski, *Traveling the Eastern Line*, 18.

246. U.S. Senate, "Landmark Legislation."

247. American Battlefield Trust, "Reconstruction."

248. U.S. Senate, "Landmark Legislation."

249. American History Central Online, "Thirteenth Amendment."

250. American History Central Online, "Fourteenth Amendment."

251. Ibid.

252. National Constitution Center Online, "Reconstruction Amendments."

253. PocketSights, "Longwood Progressive Friends Meetinghouse."

254. "Longwood Progressive Meegtinghouse," *Delaware County Times*.

Chapter 5

255. Wikipedia, "Hinsonville."

256. Russo and Russo, *Hinsonville*, 2.

257. Ibid., 16.

258. Kashatus, *Just Over the Line*, 92.

259. Kashatus and Stavenski, *Traveling the Eastern Line*, 19.

260. Gooch, *Hinsonville's Heroes*, 15.

261. Russo and Russo, *Hinsonville*, 14.

262. Ibid., 16.

263. Ibid., 35.

264. Ibid., 19.

265. Berlin, *Generations of Captivity*, 243.

266. Schultz, "Hosanna Church."

267. Russo and Russo, *Hinsonville*, 136.

268. Schultz, "Hosanna Church."

269. Russo and Russo, *Hinsonville*, 135.

270. Ibid., 100.

271. History, "54th Massachusetts."

272. Berlin, *Generations of Captivity*, 255.

273. Kashatus, *Just Over the Line*, 69.

274. Gooch, *Hinsonville's Heroes*, 15–16.

275. History, "54th Massachusetts."

276. Ibid.

277. Ibid.
278. Ibid.
279. Ibid.
280. Ibid.
281. Ibid.

Chapter 6

282. Dowling, *History of Churches*, 83.
283. Russo and Russo, *Hinsonville*, 50.
284. Kashatus, *Just Over the Line*, 56.
285. Russo and Russo, *Hinsonville*, 50.
286. Uzelac, "African Americans."
287. Barber, "Legacy of Slavery," n.p.
288. Dowling, *History of Churches*, 83.
289. Nielson, "Hosanna."
290. Russo and Russo, *Hinsonville*, 56.
291. Uzelac, "African Americans."
292. Ibid.
293. U.S. National Park Service, "54th Massachusetts."
294. Uzelac, "African Americans."
295. Russo and Russo, *Hinsonville*, 45.
296. Lawrence, "Methodist Church, Slavery and Politics," 1.
297. Ibid., 10.
298. Wikipedia, "Big August Quarterly."
299. Mother Africa Union Church, "August Quarterly."
300. Ibid.
301. Wikipedia, "Peter Spencer."
302. Ibid.
303. Uzelac, "African Americans."
304. Barber, "Legacy of Slavery."
305. Kashatus and Stavenski, *Traveling the Eastern Line*, 21.
306. Dedication of an Official State Historical Marker Honoring Hosanna African Union Methodist Protestant Church.
307. Toni Morrison Society, "Bench by the Road."
308. Ibid.
309. Lincoln University, "Friends of Hosanna."
310. Russo and Russo, *Hinsonville*, 54.

Chapter 7

311. Russo and Russo, *Hinsonville*, 49.
312. Lincoln University, "History."
313. Encyclopedia.com, "Lincoln University."
314. Dowling, *History of Churches*, 84.
315. Bond, *Education for Freedom*, 210.
316. Russo and Russo, *Hinsonville*, 97.
317. Levister, Zoom call with the author.
318. Russo and Russo, *Hinsonville*, 100.
319. Ibid., 102.
320. Murray, *Proud Shoes*, 107.
321. Holmes, "Amos Brothers."
322. Russo and Russo, *Hinsonville*, 29.
323. Ibid., 115.
324. Gooch, *Africa's Lands*, 1.
325. Lincoln University, "History."
326. Ibid.
327. Battaglia, "Freedom at Lincoln."
328. Ibid.
329. Berlin, *Generations of Captivity*, 242.
330. Wikipedia, "Anti-Literacy Laws."
331. Wikipedia, "Freedman's Aid Society."
332. Lincoln University, "History."
333. Lincoln University, "New Book."
334. Battaglia, "Freedom at Lincoln."
335. Ibid.
336. Berlin, *Generations of Captivity*, 254.

Appendix A

337. Lincoln University, "History of Firsts."

Appendix B

338. Hollingsworth, "Port of Sanctuary," 41.
339. Karasu, "Black Artists."

340. Ibid.
341. Ibid.
342. Ibid.
343. Sudarkasa, *Barnes Bond Connection*, 8.
344. Levister, Zoom call with the author.
345. Wikipedia, "*The Art of the Steal*."
346. Ibid.
347. Saint Joseph's University, "Barnes Horticulture Certificate."
348. Rein, email to the author.

BIBLIOGRAPHY

African American Civil War Museum. "On the Tradition of Watch Night." December 31, 2012. www.afroamcivilwar.org.

American Battlefield Trust. "Reconstruction Amendments." www.battlefields.org.

American History Central Online. "Emancipation Proclamation." www.americanhistorycentral.com.

———. "Fourteenth Amendment." www.americanhistorycentral.com.

———. "Fugitive Slave Act of 1850." www.americanhistorycentral.com.

———. "Fugitive Slave Act of 1850 Facts." www.americancentralhistory.com.

———. "Fugitive Slave Act of 1793." www.americanhistorycentral.com.

———. "Fugitive Slave Act of 1793 Facts." www.americanhistorycentral.com.

———. "Thirteenth Amendment." www.americancentralhistory.com.

Barber, Chris. "Legacy of Slavery Remains in Black Churches." *Southern Chester County Weeklies*, April 18, 2013. www.southernchestercountyweeklies.com.

Battaglia, Emily. "Freedom at Lincoln University: It's History and Legacy." Pennsylvania Center for the Book, n.d. www.pabook.libraries.psu.edu.

Berlin, Ira. *Generations of Captivity: A History of African-American Slaves.* Cambridge, MA: Belknap Press of Harvard University Press, 2003.

Blockson, Charles L. *Hippocrene Guide to the Underground Railroad.* New York: Hippocrene Books Inc., 1994.

Bond, Horace Mann. *Education for Freedom: A History of Lincoln University.* Princeton, NJ: Princeton University Press for Lincoln University, 1976.

Bordewich, Fergus M. *Bound for Canaan: The Underground Railroad and the War for the Soul of America.* New York: Harper Collins Publishers, 2005.

Bryn Mawr. "Quakers and Slavery: Organizations." www.web.tricolib. brynmawr.edu.

Bulletin for the 150th Anniversary Celebration. Kennett Square, PA: Longwood Progressive Friends Meetinghouse, May 22, 2005. (Housed at the Chester County History Center, box "Society of Friends, Meetings L–M," West Chester, PA.)

Calarco, Tom. *People of the Underground Railroad: A Biographical Dictionary.* Westport, CT: Greenwood Press, 2008.

Carey, Brycchan, and Geoffrey Plank, eds. *Quakers and Abolition.* Urbana: University of Illinois Press, 2018.

Dedication of an Official State Historical Marker Honoring Hosanna African Union Methodist Protestant Church, Sunday, May 9, 1992. (This program is housed at the Chester County History Center.)

Delaware County Times. "Longwood Progressive Meetinghouse and Cemetery Honored by National Park Service." January 20, 2015.

Densmore, Christopher. "Be Ye Therefore Perfect: Anti-Slavery and the Origins of the Yearly Meeting of Progressive Friends in Chester County, Pennsylvania." *Quaker History* 93, no. 2 (2004): 28–46. www. marlboroughmeeting.org.

———. "Truth for Authority, Not Authority for Truth." Kennett Underground Railroad Center. May 22, 2005. www.kennettundergroundrr.org.

Dixon, Mark E. "How This Civil War-Era Man Helped Create Modern Taxes." *Maine Line Today*, March 3, 2016. www.mainlinetoday.com.

Dowling, Iris G., ed. *History of Churches & Worship Groups in the Oxford Area.* Oxford, PA: Oxford Area Historical Association, 2012.

Dugan, Mary L., and Ella J. Sestrich. *East Linden Street: A History—Abolition, Industry & Diversity in Kennett Square, PA.* Kennett Square, PA: Kennett Underground Railroad Center, 2008.

Ecenbarger, William. *Walkin' the Line.* New York: M. Evans and Company Inc., 2000.

Encyclopedia.com. "Lincoln University." www.encyclopedia.com.

ExplorePAHistory.com "Christiana Riot Historical Marker—Behind the Marker." www.explorepahistory.com.

Gara, Larry. "Friends and the Underground Railroad." *Quaker History* 51, no. 1 (1962): 3–19. www.jstor.org.

Garrison, Webb. *Amazing Women of the Civil War—Fascinating True Stories of Women Who Made a Difference.* Nashville, TN: Rutledge Hill Press, 1999.

Gooch, Cheryl Renee. *Hinsonville's Heroes: Black Civil War Soldiers of Chester County, Pennsylvania.* Charleston, SC: The History Press, 2018.

———. *On Africa's Lands: The Forgotten Stories of Two Lincoln Educated Missionaries in Liberia.* Lincoln University, PA: Lincoln University Press, 2014.

Haas, Kimberly. "Imagining a Route to Freedom Aboard the Underground Railroad." Hidden City. www.hiddencityphila.org.

Harris, Randolph J., and Leroy T. Hopkins Jr. "Resistance at Christiana." Underground Railroad Origins in Pennsylvania. December 2016. www.undergroundrroriginspa.org.

Historical Society of Pennsylvania Online. "Pennsylvania Abolition Society in Context: A Timeline." www.hsp.org.

History. "The 54th Massachusetts Infantry." April 14, 2010. www.history.com.

Hoffman, Steven. "Kennett's Underground Railroad Center." *Chester County Press,* June 13, 2017. www.chestercounty.com.

Hollingsworth, Charles H. "Port of Sanctuary: The Aesthetic of the African/African-American and the Barnes Foundation." *Art Foundation* 47, no. 6 (1994): 41–42.

Holmes, Kristen E. "Amos Brothers Get Their Due for the Founding of Lincoln University." *Inquirer,* June 16, 2014. www.inquirer.com.

James, Arthur E. *The Potters and Potteries of Chester County, Pennsylvania.* Exton, PA: Schiffer Publishing Limited, 1978.

Jordan, Ryan P. *Slavery and the Meetinghouse: The Quakers and the Abolitionist Dilemma, 1820–1865.* Bloomington: Indiana University Press, 2007.

Karasu, Sylvia R. "Black Artists, Racial Equality, and Dr. Albert C. Barnes." *Psychology Today,* August 11, 2020. www.psychologytoday.com.

Kashatus, William C. *Just Over the Line: Chester County and the Underground Railroad.* West Chester, PA: Chester County Historical Society, 2002.

Kashatus, William C., and Anthony J. Stavenski, eds. *Traveling the Eastern Line: Student Essays on Southeastern Pennsylvania's Underground Railroad.* West Chester, PA: Star Printing Inc., 2002.

Kopaczewski, James. "Christiana Riot Trial." Encyclopedia of Greater Philadelphia. www.philadelphiaencyclopedia.org.

Landefeld, William R., Jr. *The Changing Boundaries of Pennsylvania from 1493–1921.* Kinzers, PA: Davco Advertising Inc., 2009.

Lawrence, Brian D. "The Relationship Between the Methodist Church, Slavery and Politics, 1784–1844" Master's thesis, Rowan University, 2018.

Leslie, William R. "The Pennsylvania Fugitive Slave Act of 1828." *Journal of Southern History* 18, no. 4 (1952): 429–45.

Lewis, Graceanna. "Recollections of Anti-Slavery Times—Dr. Bartholomew Fussell." *Friend: A Religious and Literary Journal* 69, no. 40 (1896): 313–20. www.play.google.com.

Lincoln University. "The Friends of Hosanna at Lincoln University Erects 'Bench by the Road.'" September 21, 2015. www.lincoln.edu.

———. "The History of Lincoln University." www.lincoln.edu.

———. "Lincoln's History of Firsts." July 15, 2017. www.lincoln.edu.

———. "New Book on First Lincoln Graduates Chronicles Missionary Efforts in Liberia." June 3, 2014. www.lincoln.edu.

Lucas, Loraine. "Abraham Lincoln's Quaker Roots Traced to the Barnards of Chester County and The Kennett Underground Railroad." Chester County Day, 2016. www.chestercountyhospital.org.

Maddox, Lucy. *The Parker Sisters—A Border Kidnapping.* Philadelphia, PA: Temple University Press, 2016.

Melton, J. Gordon. "African American Methodism in the M.E. Tradition: The Case of Sharp Street (Baltimore)." *North Star* 8, no. 2 (Spring 2005): 1–19. www.princeton.edu.

Mother Africa Union Church. "What Is August Quarterly." www.motherafricanunion.org.

Murray, Pauli. *Proud Shoes: The Story of an American Family.* Boston, MA: Beacon Press, 1999.

Nathan, Roger E. *East of the Mason-Dixon Line: A History of the Delaware Boundaries.* Dover, DE: Delaware Heritage Press, 2000.

National Constitution Center Online. "The Reconstruction Amendments." www.constitutioncenter.org.

Nielson, Euell A. "Hosanna African American Union Methodist Protestant Church (1843)." November 2, 2015. www.blackpast.org.

Nuermberger, Ruth Ketring. *The Free Produce Movement: A Quaker Protest Against Slavery.* New York: AMS Press, 1942.

Ohio History Central. "American Anti-Slavery Society." www.ohiohistorycentral.org.

Patten, William C. *The Anti-Slavery Movement in Chester County, Pennsylvania.* Newark: University of Delaware Press, 1963.

Pisasale, Gene. "Pathway to Freedom: Kennett Square's Underground Railroad." *Daily Local News,* May 4, 2012. www.dailylocal.com.

PocketSights. "East Linden Street, Kennett Square, Pennsylvania, 19348." www.pocketsights.com.

———. "John (1786–1880) and Hannah (née Peirce, 1797–1876) Cox Residence c. 1797." www.pocketsights.com.

———. "Kennett Area Underground Railroad Self-Guided Driving Tour." www.pocketsights.com.

———. "Longwood Progressive Friends Meetinghouse and Cemetery c. 1855." www.pocketsights.com.

Reynolds, David S. *Mightier Than the Sword: Uncle Tom's Cabin and the Battle for America*. New York: W.W. Norton & Company, 2011.

Rice, Anthony. *A Legacy Transformed: The Christiana Riot I Historical Memory*. Bethlehem, PA: Lehigh University Press, 2012.

Russo, Marianne H., and Paul A. Russo. *Hinsonville, A Community at the Crossroads: The Story of a Nineteenth Century African American Village*. Selinsgrove, PA: Susquehanna University Press, 2005.

Saint Joseph's University. "Barnes Horticulture Certificate Program." www.sju.edu.

Schultz, Elizabeth. "Hosanna Church: The Last Building in Hinsonville." Pennsylvania Historic Preservation. March 26, 2014. www.pahistoricpreservation.com.

Slavery Monuments. "Harriett Tubman Memorial Plaque." www.slaverymonuments.org.

Smedley, R.C. *History of the Underground Railroad in Chester and Neighboring Counties in Pennsylvania (1883)*. Mechanicsburg, PA: Stackpole Books, 2005.

Stokes, Isabella. "Quote About Peoples Hall." www.peoples-hall.org.

Sudarkasa, Niara, ed. *The Barnes Bond Connection*. Lincoln University, PA: Lincoln University Press, 1995.

Switala, William J. *Underground Railroad in Pennsylvania*. 2nd ed. Mechanicsburg, PA: Stackpole Books, 2008.

Taylor, Francis C. *The Trackless Trail*. Kennett Square, PA: KNA Publishing, 1976.

———. *The Trackless Trail Leads On: An Exploration of Conductors and Their Stations*. West Chester, PA: Graphics Standard, 1995.

Toni Morrison Society. "Bench by the Road Project." www.tonimorrisonsociety.org.

Turner, Edward R. "The Abolition of Slavery in Pennsylvania." *Pennsylvania Magazine of History and Biography* 36, no. 2 (1912): 129–42. www.jstor.org.

———. "The First Abolition Society in the United States." *Pennsylvania Magazine of History and Biography* 36, no. 1 (1912): 92–109. www.jstor.org.

———. "The Underground Railroad in Pennsylvania." *Pennsylvania Magazine of History and Biography* 36, no. 3 (1912): 309–18. www.jstor.org.

U.S. National Archives and Records Administration. "Transcript of the Emancipation Proclamation." www.ourdocuments.gov.

U.S. National Park Service. "Aboard the Underground Railroad—Oakdale." www.nps.gov.

———. "54ᵗʰ Massachusetts Regiment." www.nps.gov.

U.S. Senate. "Landmark Legislation: Thirteenth, Fourteenth, & Fifteenth Amendments." www.senate.gov.

Uzelac, Coni Porter. "African Americans in Chester County." www.files.usgwarchives.net.

Wahl, Albert J. "The Progressive Friends of Longwood." *Bulletin of Friends Historical Association* 42, no. 1 (1953): 13–32. www.jstor.org.

Wikipedia. "American Anti-Slavery Society." www.en.wikipedia.org.

———. "Anti-Literacy Laws in the United States." www.en.wikipedia.org.

———. "*The Art of the Steal* (2009 film)." www.en.wikipedia.org.

———. "Bartholomew Fussell." www.en.wikipedia.org.

———. "Big August Quarterly." www.en.wikipedia.org.

———. "Ercildoun, Pennsylvania." www.en.wikipedia.org.

———. "Frederick Douglass." www.en.wikipedia.org.

———. "Freedmen's Aid Society." www.en.wikipedia.org.

———. "Hinsonville." www.en.wikipedia.org.

———. "History of Slavery in Pennsylvania." www.en.wikipedia.org.

———. "John Greenleaf Whittier." www.en.wikipedia.org.

———. "Pennsylvania Abolition Society." www.en.wikipedia.org.

———. "Peter Spencer (religious leader)." www.en.wikipedia.org.

———. "Sojourner Truth." www.en.wikipedia.org.

———. "Susan B. Anthony." www.en.wikipedia.org.

Wiley, Samuel T. *Biographical and Portrait Cyclopedia of Chester County, Pennsylvania, Comprising a Historical Sketch of the County*. Edited by Winfield Scott Garner. Philadelphia, PA: Gresham Publishing Company, 1893.

Wilkinson, Norman B. "The Philadelphia Free Produce Attack Upon Slavery." *Pennsylvania Magazine of History and Biography* 66, no. 3 (1942): 294–313. www.jstor.org.

Yarnall, Howard E. "Longwood Meeting." *Bulletin of Friends Historical Association* 17, no. 2 (1928): 49–54. www.jstor.org.

Newspapers

All articles utilized from the following newspapers have been clipped from the original newspaper, mounted on cardboard and are stored at the Chester County History Center. There are no page numbers.

Coatesville Weekly Times (Coatesville, PA), November 21, 1837.
Daily Local News (West Chester, PA), March 14, 1925.
Kennett News and Advertiser (Kennett Square, PA), February 18, 1942.
Liberator (Boston, MA), September 13, 1834.
Pennsylvania Freeman (Philadelphia, PA), September 6, 1849.
———. October 3, 1850.
Philadelphia Record (Philadelphia, PA), May 6, 1906.
Register and Examiner (West Chester, PA), February 28, 1837.

Zoom Call

Levister, Dr. Ernest C. Zoom call with author. May 17, 2021.

Email

Rein, William. Email to author. July 22, 2021.

ABOUT THE AUTHOR

Mark Lanyon's twenty-plus-year career in behavioral health was launched when he was studying for his Master of Human Services degree at Lincoln University (LU '98). During his career, Mark supervised and/or directed numerous behavioral health programs in settings such as the prison system, probation and parole system, hospitals and inpatient and outpatient behavioral health treatment programs.

Mark was often requested to provide training for the Delaware Family Court, the Wilmington Police Academy, Wilmington Hospital Programs, Division of Family Services (DFS), Delaware Technical College programs, New Castle County Police and the University of Delaware.

Over the past ten years, Mark has been involved with his personal genealogy research. This research resulted in him becoming a member of a variety of societies and organizations: Sons of the American Revolution (SAR; two of his ancestors fought in the American Revolution); the General Society of Mayflower Descendants (seven of his ancestors were passengers on the *Mayflower*); the St. Andrew's Society (Philadelphia; one of his ninth-great-grandfathers emigrated from Scotland); the Society of St. George (Philadelphia); and the Royal Society of St. George (London, another ninth-great-grandfather emigrated from England).

Since retiring, Mark has been able to concentrate on his research of the rich history present in Southern Chester County, Pennsylvania. His research covered slavery, the Underground Railroad, the abolitionist movement, the Longwood Progressive Friends Meeting and the founding of Lincoln University.

Mark is excited to share his research of the events, people and places that make Southern Chester County, Pennsylvania, the crucible of freedom.

Visit us at
www.historypress.com

CPSIA information can be obtained
at www.ICGtesting.com
Printed in the USA
BVHW060923020222
627878BV00002B/144